Pie Town Woman

PIE TOWN WOMAN

The Hard Life and Good Times

of a New Mexico Homesteader

JOAN MYERS

UNIVERSITY OF NEW MEXICO PRESS / ALBUQUERQUE

First edition

Second paperbound printing, 2003

Library of Congress Cataloging-in-Publication Data

Myers, Joan, 1944–
    Pie Town woman : the hard life and good times of a New Mexico
homesteader / Joan Myers.— 1st ed.
        p. cm.
    Includes bibliographical references.
    ISBN 0-8263-2283-2 (alk. paper) — ISBN 0-8263-2284-0 (pbk. : alk.
paper)
    1. Caudill, Doris. 2. Caudill, Doris—Pictorial works. 3. Pie Town
(N.M.)—Biography. 4. Rural women—New Mexico—Pie Town—Social
conditions. 5. Rural women—New Mexico—Pie Town—Pictorial works. 6.
Depressions—1929—New Mexico. 7. Depressions—1929—New
Mexico—Pictorial works. 8. Documentary photography—New Mexico.   I.
Title.
  F804.P54 M94 2001
  978.9'93—dc21

                                                                2001000379

Design: *Mina Yamashita*

CONTENTS

ACKNOWLEDGMENTS

This is Doris's story, and my first and greatest debt is to her. It is an honor and a considerable pleasure to tell her story. At our first meeting, we enjoyed each other's company and agreed that her story needed to be told. From that moment on, she took me into her life. She answered countless questions, provided precious family photographs, housed and fed me. She is one of the most generous people I've had the opportunity to meet. My only regret is that her health did not allow her to accompany me on a final visit back to Pie Town.

I am grateful to the Library of Congress for providing the beautifully printed Russell Lee photographs used for the reproductions in this book. In choosing the images for this first section of the book, I have focused on images of Doris and her family. Interestingly, her family appears so frequently in the Lee images that this selection does not violate the overall integrity of Lee's body of work. I have included a couple of images of Pie Town itself, even though her family does not appear in them, since they were frequent visitors to town despite the eleven-mile journey over rough roads from Divide, where they lived. I hope that this selection of photographs, by concentrating on Doris's family, will serve to personalize images that have become abstract, make "homey" photographs that are now expensive works of art, and generally question the way we look at historical photographs. Although these images provide valuable historical information for scholars, they are also photographs of individuals, all with their own stories to tell.

Captions for the Lee photographs are my own. I have based them loosely on Jean Lee's captions, which accompany the photographs at the Library of Congress, but I have made changes and added some material, including the names of people who were not identified in the original captions.

Jean Lee offered me invaluable information about her working relationship with her husband Russell and a first-hand account of how the Pie Town pictures were conceived and taken. I enjoyed our interview immensely and wish we might have met again before her death a few months later.

Many people helped me understand what life was like in the homesteading era of Pie Town. Among them were Loraine Burns, Colita Schalbar,

Sam McKee, and Roy McKee. Roy's daughter, Kathryn McKee Roberts, was especially helpful; she has become the town's historian, publishing a fine book, *From the Top of the Mountain: Pie Town, New Mexico, and Neighbors!* I would like to also thank Joan Jensen for her scholarship, enthusiasm, and understanding.

For perspective on modern Catron County, I would like to thank Jackie Barrington, Kathy Knapp, and Carl Moore.

I am especially grateful to Tommy Padilla, brand inspector for Catron County, who allowed me access to the land that the community of Divide once occupied. I spent several days there photographing the remains of structures that belonged to the Caudills and their neighbors. The site has been undisturbed for many years behind a locked gate, observed only by a few cows and horses. With Tommy Padilla's help and Doris's map, I could find where all the houses, school house, and cemetery once stood.

The impetus for meeting Doris came from Mary Powell and Marta Weigle; each subsequently offered encouragement and helpful suggestions on the manuscript. Mary Powell also accompanied me on a trip to Pie Town, providing both moral support and assistance with camera gear, and later offering additional encouragement and much needed counsel. Good advice and manuscript suggestions also came from Martha Sandweiss and Brent Jarrett. Steve Yates, curator of photography at the Museum of Fine Arts, Santa Fe, New Mexico, provided encouragement and the use of the museum archives on Russell Lee and Pie Town. A special thanks goes to Mike Webb, who printed many of the silver prints of my images and Doris Caudill's snapshots used in the book reproductions.

Beth Hadas, my editor at UNM Press, was supportive and encouraging throughout this project from its inception. Her editing was invaluable. Her patience and belief in the book over the more than five-year period that the book was in progress meant a great deal to me. Mina Yamashita designed the book with skill and passion. Finally, my husband Bernie López supported me throughout this project, reading the manuscript several times and, despite all evidence to the contrary, encouraging me to write, as well as to photograph.

PHOTOGRAPHS BY RUSSELL LEE

Business section of Pie Town, June 1940, as it looked when Russell and Jean Lee arrived.
LC-USF 34-36796-D

Joe A. Keele, president of the Farm Bureau, carrying a load of groceries from the mercantile store he owned with Harmon L. Craig. / LC-USF 34-36771-D

The "stage," which daily brought in the mail, freight, express, and passengers.
LC-USF 34-36739-D

Dike and road leading from Pie Town to Divide. / LC-USF 34-36640-D

*Dugout home of the Caudills with Doris standing by a pickup truck that Faro
took in trade for lumber cut on the homestead. / LC-USF 34-36627-D*

*Faro and Doris Caudill with their daughter Josie in their dugout home
close to Alegra Mountain. / LC-USF 34-36560-D*

Doris ironing. / LC-USF 34-36581-D

Doris and Josie in their dugout. Behind them is their radio, one of the few in the community. / LC-USF 33-12735-M4

Josie combing her hair.
LC-USF 34-36757-D

Josie and her friend Bill Fowler playing with goats at an all-day Sunday birthday party. / LC-USF 33-12754-M3

Josie looking over a slab fence on her family's homestead.
LC-USF 34-36542-D

Faro. / LC-USF 33-12753-M5

Faro coming up out of his dugout. / LC-USF 34-36583-D

Doris milking. / LC-USF 33-12750-M5

Doris placing milk into a homemade cooling box. Damp cloths are wrapped around the buckets and jars of milk, and rapid evaporation in the open-air produces sufficient cooling to keep milk from spoiling. / LC-USF 34-36529-D

*Faro planting beans. The block of wood dragging after the planter is a
homemade contrivance for smoothing out soil after seeds have been planted.*
LC-USF 33-12718-M5

Doris setting out cabbage plants in her garden. / LC-USF 34-36585-D

Doris patching her husband's trousers. / LC-USF 34-36618-D

Doris looking at canned goods in her storage cellar. / LC-USF 34-36551-D

Faro drawing water. He will haul it five miles back to his house.
LC-USF 34-36571-D

Water witch Fred Caudill, Faro's father, holding a green forked stick
firmly in his hands. The stick twists in the general direction of water.
LC-USF 33-12750-M2

Neighbor John Adams helping Faro tear down the Caudill dugout.
LC-USF 34-36853-D

Doris and Josie carrying household equipment to their new dugout.
LC-USF 33-12768-M5

*Dragging a log half a mile from the old dugout to be used
in building the new dugout. / LC-USF 33-12768-M3*

*The Caudill family eating dinner in the open on the day they were
moving their dugout. / LC-USF 33-12706-M1*

Faro and his neighbor John Adams building the dugout. / *LC-USF 34-36905-D*

New Caudill dugout near their well. / *LC-USF 34-36825-D*

Homesteaders visiting all day Sunday to celebrate a birthday.
LC-USF 33-12736-M3

*Doris on the front steps of Dick and Ozella Fowler's house, a couple of miles
away from the Caudill homestead. Oleta and Molly Fowler look at her.*
LC-USF 33-1222753-M1

Josie cutting pie in the Fowlers' house where several families
celebrate a birthday. / LC-USF 34-36591-D

*4-H Club members giving their pledge. Doris, second from end on right,
is their leader. / LC-USF 34-36899-D*

Joe Beeson, president of the Literary Society, holding the lamp for Doris,
secretary, during a song at the Literary Society. / LC-USF 34-36696-D

Farmers and their families enjoying the Literary Society meeting.
LC-USF 34-36661-D

A hand of poker at a forty-two party at neighbor Les Thomas's house.
LC-USF 34-36637-D

Josie asleep at forty-two party. / LC-USF 34-36638-D

Dancing the Paul Jones at Bill Staggs's all-night party. / LC-USF 34-36974-D

The men have a bottle of beer at the square dance. / LC-USF 34-36898-D

*Spectators, including Doris and Josie, at the square dance. Women and small
children sit on one side of the room the men and older boys on the other.*
LC-USF 34-36808-D

Former Texas sharecropper Olie McKee dances a jig. / LC-USF 34-36912-D

Etta Mae McKee, left, dances with Edna Dean Woolery at Bill Staggs's party. Ruth Thomas stands near wall. Edna Dean's fancy bow and dress identify her as a visitor. / LC-USF 34-36870-D

PIE TOWN WOMAN

A WOMAN OF NEW MEXICO

In 1984, I accidentally found myself in Pie Town, New Mexico. That year, after visiting my brother in Arizona, I returned home to Santa Fe via Springerville and Magdalena. It was fall and the aspens had just begun to turn in the high altitudes of the Fort Apache Indian Reservation in the White Mountains of Arizona. I camped for a night under a great bowl of stars, grilled a steak by flashlight, then fell asleep smelling ponderosa pine and wood smoke. Next morning, heading east on Highway 60, I drove into Pie Town.

Pie Town. Seeing the name on the highway sign, I put my foot on the brake and slowed down. The name made me think of potluck suppers, Sunday school, Main Street parades and moms who stay home to bake bread and drive their kids to piano lessons after school. The name conjured up a past innocence, a destiny of family and community roots, a timeless place.

I remembered the name Pie Town, vaguely, from a 1941 *U.S. Camera* article with photographs by Russell Lee. Russell Lee worked for the history division of the Farm Security Administration, the FSA, from 1936 to 1942. He and his wife Jean traveled eleven months of the year photographing the effects of the New Deal agricultural policies on people who had suffered through the Depression and Dust Bowl. When the Lees arrived in Pie Town in mid-April, 1940, they were charmed by the struggles and spirit of the remote New Mexican town with the whimsical name. They decided to take extra time and record what they saw.

When I drove into Pie Town that morning, I could not recall many specific images. All I knew was that Lee had succeeded in making a set of pictures that typified the struggles of families to eke out a living in the difficult years between the Depression and World War II. I did remember a photograph of a woman looking proudly at one of her jars of canned goods. The woman's name, I was to learn, was Doris Caudill. In all, I found out later, Lee took more than six hundred photographs in the Pie Town area, and Doris and her family appeared in over a hundred of them.

That morning I could well have missed Pie Town altogether. A sip of coffee at the wrong time and I might not have paid attention to the few buildings that lined the highway—the Break 21 Café, a tiny post office with a handmade sign, and a couple of small wooden houses festooned with discarded appliances and parts from rusty pickups. Curious, I left the highway and drove through the oldest part of Pie Town, along a dirt road that had been the main highway before a bypass was paved in 1957. There were no traffic lights. I stopped at the only stop sign, but it seemed more of a formality than a necessity. A three-legged dog eyed me without interest and hopped across the intersection diagonally.

Most houses were unpainted and boarded up. A few homes were occupied and landscaped with gardens of blue and purple bottles set on fence posts. In 1935, about three hundred families lived in Pie Town. Today, fewer than a hundred residents live within a twenty-mile radius. A small, white, clapboard rectangular building had a sign reading "Community Center," but it was closed. Nearby was a small park with seesaws, swings, and a basketball hoop, but it was empty. Both the Baptist and Latter-day Saints churches looked in good condition and offered regular services, but surely neither could boast a large congregation, guessing from the size of the town.

I stopped in the café for a cup of coffee and chatted with Lester Jackson, an ex-Marine who had bought the place with his wife Emily, in February 1976. He was a cheerful, stocky man with tattoos on both arms, short gray hair and a small mustache. He told me he had moved to Pie Town after four tours of duty in Vietnam, opened the café and started baking pies. He cut me a generous slice of his apple pie, which was flaky and delicious. A plate on the wall indicated that the Jacksons had made 17,718 pies since they bought the place.

When I complimented his pie, Lester reached under the counter and brought up a well-worn copy of a 1983 article from the *Albuquerque Journal*. A photo showed Lester standing behind Ed Jones, the previous town pie maker. Though Lester was a relative newcomer to town, he showed it to me with the pleasure of a man who drew sustenance from a long-simmering and rich history that now included him. The article also included several Russell Lee photographs, including *Jigger at Pie Town*, perhaps the most famous image from the series that Lee made of a neighborhood square dance in 1940. In the picture, a man is dancing with a can in one hand and his right foot raised high off the ground while a group of women watch intently from their seats on the couch behind him.

Post office in
Pie Town today
Photo: Joan Myers

What had happened to the homesteaders Lee photographed? Where was Doris Caudill, the woman who looked so proudly at her canning accomplishments? Was she at the square dance, too? Where had the square dancers gone? Certainly they were no longer to be found in town or on the farms they had worked so hard to establish. My chance stopping in Pie Town in 1984 set me to wondering about Lee's photographs. The contrast between Pie Town then and Pie Town now intrigued me. The questions nagged at the borders of my consciousness for several years.

By chance, in 1993, Mary Powell, a friend of mine and publisher of Ancient City Press, showed me a letter written by a former resident of Pie Town. It was occasioned by her publication of the book *Women of New Mexico: Depression Era Images* and was addressed to the book's author, Marta Weigle. The letter was written by a Doris Jackson, formerly Doris Caudill, and began:

> *I am writing you because I too am a woman of New Mexico.*
> *In 1930–32 I spent each summer traveling with George Mickey,*

a Church of Christ minister who spent each summer holding meetings in different communities, at Pie Town, and community schoolhouses there in Catron County. His oldest daughter was my best friend. I don't know anything about writing and can't spell my own name but never the less I wrote in longhand about 46 pages of my life at Pie Town. . . .

When Russell Lee came out to take his pictures, he was in my home many times. He loved to follow my daughter Josie around to make pictures of her doing what she normally did each day at play. . . .

I told Russell about a square dance we were having at a neighbor's house & invited he and Jean to go. He did & got a lot of very fine pictures. One was McKee doing a jig. Another was the kids asleep on the bed. My Josie was the first one next to the camera. You can see her big feet better than her face. . . .

Sorry to take up so much of your time but when I get started thinking of the Pie Town years I don't want to stop talking. We were dirt poor but we didn't know it. We were happy and made our own fun.[1]

In her forty-six-page memoir, which I eventually received, Doris had written down some of her life and filled in some of the spaces that preceded Lee's involvement. In Sweetwater, Texas, her childhood home, where she lived in a clapboard house, she married and later gave birth to her daughter, Josie. Doris left that house when she married and then moved to a dugout in the small settlement of Divide in west central New Mexico. The post office for Divide and neighboring communities was in nearby Pie Town, and everyone who used that post office called Pie Town home. She and her then husband Faro lived on their homestead there for a little more than ten years. In her own handwriting, she detailed the daily life of those years, as well as some of the special events that she remembered.

Her letter triggered more questions and reminded me of those that my short visit to Pie Town had raised. What had happened to her since 1940? How could being "dirt poor" lead to such joyful memories? How did Doris's feelings and memories about Pie Town compare to Lee's photographic observations and how did she feel about those photographs now? Lee had photographed a few moments in the daily lives of some of the residents of Pie Town in mid-1940, but each person photographed had a life that extended beyond the frame into the past and the future. How had the experience in Pie Town affected the rest of Doris's life? I wanted to meet her, to hear her story, and to assess the accuracy of Lee's larger-than-life photographs.

With the encouragement of both Mary Powell and Marta Weigle, I went to Doris's present home in Cascade Locks, Oregon, to take her picture and get to know her.

Doris's house in Oregon is only a few blocks from the broad flow of the Columbia River. If it is not raining, you can walk to the riverbank and look at the old canal and locks. In 1896, the now historic Cascade Rapids shipping locks allowed the first heavy shipping to inland Oregon and Washington. A small park now encompasses the canal and locks, and near the edge of the locks local Indians from the Warm Springs Reservation net-fish for salmon.

This place is like the bottom of the sea, submerged and damp, a world away from the rabbitbrush and dust and blue sky that once made up Doris's home in arid New Mexico. Here in Oregon people use the expression "Not a sky in the cloud." When Doris looks out her window she cannot see farther than the house across the street for all the moist air, the dogwood, sumac, the rhododendron and azalea bushes, and the cloud shadows. When the mist or rains settle in she sees no farther than the water crisscrossing her windowpanes.

Her husband Jack is not well. That is why Doris cannot return to the places of her past and why I have come here today. She would have preferred to meet me in Pie Town. She thought of returning every so often over the last fifty years, but time has passed and she has not done it. Then Jack had a couple of strokes, and she needs to be with him. When he has trouble, he has to go to the Veterans

Administration Hospital in Portland, more than an hour's drive away. She worries, of course, especially since she cannot drive so well anymore and often has to get someone else to take him in to the doctor. She has had a couple of small strokes herself, but she had to tell me this; I would never have guessed it from being around her.

When I call her the night before our first meeting, she asks me to show up early in the morning, and I suggest nine o'clock.

"Hey, kid, I'm up at four-thirty in the morning and by nine I'll have my nails all chewed down waiting for you."

We compromise at eight-thirty, and when I drive up she throws open the front door and comes out on the porch before I have time to get out of my car.

"Hey, what's up with you bringing all this rain?"

Her voice exposes her Texas childhood and the warmth of the road signs there that say, "Drive Friendly!" When I open the rear door to get the camera gear, Doris reaches in to help carry my tripod.

Preparing for this meeting, I have come to know the Lee photographs so well that I see past her at first, filling the space around her with how she looked at twenty-five. She is working outdoors, singing at the literary society meeting, directing the 4-H club or standing outside her dugout. Her husband is Faro, not Jack. Doris is twenty-five and has a young daughter.

I remember one of Russell Lee's photographs from 1940 showing Doris setting out cabbage plants in her garden. Behind her is a hand-cut picket fence. She is on her hands and knees in the dirt, lowering a spindly plant into a small depression. She wears a broad-brimmed hat, a white long-sleeved shirt, and a dark skirt. You can see the dirt on her stockings and shoes. A few feet away is a pail of hand-carried water for the new plants. She is intent on her work, her face a dark profile. You can sense the sun beating down on her back and head, and the raw earth between her fingers. The photograph is so vivid that I feel I can step inside its frame and carry on a conversation with her.

But when I walk into Doris's house in Cascade Locks and look around, nothing matches. I deposit my camera gear in a corner of the living room and turn to face her. Lee's photographic record and the woman I see before me refuse to blend into a single image. It is like meeting the woman who modeled for Leonardo's *Mona Lisa* decades after he painted her and finding she has gray hair and glasses.

Since I had told her I wanted to do a portrait, I expect her to be dressed up with her hair showing signs of a recent trip to the beauty shop. But the woman helping me with my gear has on white tennis shoes, an old sweat suit and no make-up, and her hair, on the verge of unruly, is curly and cut short. She is taller than I am and a little heavier. As we walk toward the house, she seems to have the energy of a teenager. I remind myself that she must be at least eighty; it is hard to keep in mind.

She is at once the same and different. Despite my conscious awareness of the more than fifty years that have passed, the photographs have so sliced and frozen time that I find myself fooled. I can see the younger Doris in her eyes, nose, and mouth, but I am surprised to see her wrinkles and gray hair. Next, I am caught up by her voice and motion and realize I had somehow expected her to be motionless as she was in Lee's pictures. While she hangs up my coat, I mumble a greeting to her husband who sits watching television and wonder if I am in the right house. For a moment I am overwhelmed by her aliveness. She is so much more than the images I know. Doris exceeds everything Russell Lee attributes to her, but I cannot yet take in all the difference.

As a photographer, I can laugh at my surprise. Photographs offer up convincing but prejudiced versions of the truth. Taken by an experienced photographer, photographs are visual condensations of what the photographer sees, feels, and chooses to communicate. A photographer can, by framing and selection, inflate an image beyond its actual importance and value. When Lee photographed Doris setting out cabbage plants, he also showed how harsh homesteading life could be and how determined a woman must be to feed her family. He used the images he took of Doris to distill his own feelings about families he had seen in Texas and Oklahoma struggling to survive in hard times. He used his photographic skill to do more than just depict the daily life of Pie Town.

Viewing these photographs decades later and accepting them as full and complete observations of an individual or her culture is risky business. Russell Lee's interest was not in Doris's individual dreams, hopes or struggles. He did not attempt to tell more of Doris's personal life than fit his agenda. He left many questions unexplored. How did she feel about the work she did? Did his picture depict a typical moment in her life or an unusual one? Did the family ever harvest cabbage from those plants or did the rabbits eat them all? Lee's photographs do not tell us: a life—anyone's life—is too ungainly to be contained inside a tiny rectangle.

Doris steps out the back door into the rain. She walks a few steps to her small garden and picks a pint of strawberries that would have been a freakish luxury out on her dry homestead of the '40s. Fifty-some years ago, from her Pie Town dugout, Doris could see the dust raised by visitors half an hour before they arrived; it was the lack of water that made them so visible. Shaking off the raindrops, she muses about the difference. She drains the berries in the kitchen sink and puts them in the refrigerator. Her hand movements belong to a younger woman, and she smiles often as she talks to me. Gradually I get used to the way the present imposes itself on the past, not interrupting the memories and pictures Doris and I talk about, but attaching itself to them.

She carries a basket of old photographs, small snapshots, to the table and sets it down in the middle. All the photos are black and white, and many have faded or yellowed, curling at the edges. These pictures were exposed, developed, and printed before I was born: men in their well-worn pants, children lined up in front of a school building, a smiling woman by the Model T with a dog on the hood. Anonymous faces from sixty and more years ago, they look out from past lives that have begun to disappear into the gelatin of the paper. Their faint images are catalysts for the ghosts of friends and family who, but for these photographs, are mostly gone now, or indistinct in the memory of those who knew them.

For Doris, that past time is vivid still. Long ago and yesterday are almost the same time. She tells me how dark it was that night when they waited to return home until the moon rose since they had no headlights for their Model T, and how excited she was when two members of her 4-H troop won a trip to the Chicago grain judging. She describes Josie's school and identifies each of her schoolmates by name, as if we might visit and still find them there.

Doris has kept the snapshots all these years. Like Lee's photographs, they record her time in Pie Town and many of the same people, but in a more casual, more intimate way that invites and requires more of her comments. She sifts through them and pauses every so often to laugh as she catches me up on their stories.

That big mountain, that Alegra Mountain,[2] that's where I lived, right at the foot of that mountain. That's south of Pie Town eleven miles. If I ever had the chance I'd love to take you out and show you the different places, the spot where this and that happened.[3]

She begins to show them to me. They are small photos, and their varied sizes and shapes are evidence that they were taken with different cameras, probably by different people. Doris, who did not have the money to mail the letters she wrote to her mother, did not, of course, have a camera. But others did.

These yellowed and curling photos are part of the tradition of family snapshots that began with the introduction of the Kodak camera in 1888: "You push the button; we do the rest!" By the time of the Depression, an era of sacrifices, family photographs had become a necessity. Many American families managed to afford to take them, and almost everyone was photographed. For the first time in history, people of all economic classes were able to have likenesses of their loved ones as keepsakes for themselves and for their children and grandchildren. Doris's sister had one of the inexpensive, easy-to-use box cameras, and she took pictures when she came to visit.

Doris has detailed stories to match of each of these snapshots:

This is a picture of our corral. Right here was where Dudd Hart lived. He ran off with one of the Potter girls, and they got married. They sold their place to Mr. and Mrs. Holley. Right here was

Aunt Lizzie's place and next to it was Burley Mickey, and next to Burley was Sam Mickey, and right up here was Jim Potter who had all the kids. This was between 1929 and 1936. Our community was called Divide.

It is now just past 8:30 in the morning. I am still groggy from a short night's sleep, and though we have hardly met, Doris keeps introducing me, through the snapshots, to all her family and friends. One after the other, she lifts the curling images from the basket and smiles as they plump out to form three-dimensional memories, a virtual Pie Town in her living room in Cascade Locks.

The tiny nondescript picture she shows me of a young woman standing awkwardly in front of a wooden doorway ordinarily would not have caught my attention. Without Doris, I would have no way of knowing this was Ruth Thomas as she looked on a sunny day in 1933. Doris tells me that Ruth Thomas stayed with them for two years while she went to school and that she was standing outside the Divide school building in this snapshot. Ruth was so happy living with them that she did not want to leave and return home, but she did, and not long after the war ended she married a local boy from the Divide area. Then Doris shows me a copy of one of Russell Lee's images of a Pie Town square dance. There is the same Ruth Thomas, again standing uncomfortably against a wall with two women dancing together in front of her. The stories Doris tells change how I see the images.

Doris's stories spill out beyond the images. She creates mental images for me of a room full of people listening to a Montgomery Ward's battery-powered radio, bricks that Doris's mother heated in the oven then put on the floor of their Model T to keep everyone's feet warm, two plates and three quilts from her hope chest, a five-cent Sweetwater hamburger, Sears mail-order catalogs that Doris and her husband Faro used for toilet paper. (If you do not have an income, you cannot use the catalogs to order things.) The snapshots show details of her life. Without her elaboration, they speak mainly to the people who lived in those same moments. Her stories carry me beyond her snapshots into her richly remembered past.

This girl was born there in that house. This is the Kitner place that later became the Bates place and later became where my brother moved for a year and put in a crop.

There . . . Oscar Schalbar was Aunt Lizzie's . . . well, you can read it on the back . . . Pop didn't have but six wives. That's Oscar standing in front of their house.

I look past Doris's hands into the basket with its ghostly surfaces of people's lives and listen as she shuffles the snapshots from the basket to the tabletop. I see images of husbands and wives leaning against their cars, holding their children up to the camera. I see children lined up against the wall of a schoolhouse. Stories and dreams submerged below these frozen slices of time and space surface as Doris tells her stories. I cannot keep up with the names and faces. It is like marrying into a large family and meeting all the relatives at once.

Doris hesitates, then shows me a small snapshot, and begins her narrative again. In this photo, she looks very young in a pair of trendy flowered overalls as she leans back against the log building in the photograph. She is laughing and talking, her mouth open and her eyes squinting against the sun:

Ruth Thomas

This photograph was taken the day we got to Pie Town by Sister Mickey. Brother Mickey went in to the store and asked the proprietor how to get to the home of Burley Mickey. Faro's dad, "Pop" Caudill, was standing there, and he said, "I live on the place right next to Burley, and if you'll follow me home, I'll take you right there." In the meantime we went up to have our picture made by this Pie Town sign.

Doris threatens to "talk my leg off" every time she lifts a new snapshot out of the basket. I tell her I want to hear more of the stories that go with the pictures. She reminds me of Steinbeck's Ma Joad in *Grapes of Wrath* who talks about a woman's life being "all

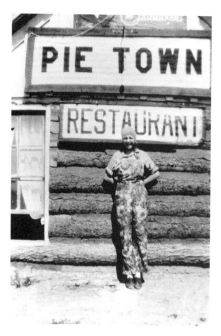

Doris in 1929

one flow, like a stream, little eddies, little waterfalls, but the river, it goes right on. Woman looks at it like that" while a man, by contrast, "lives in jerks—baby born an' a man dies, an' that's a jerk—gets a farm an' loses his farm, an' that's a jerk."[4] With the help of her snapshots, Doris is telling me her story, a particular woman's story of the frontier experience, in her own woman's voice. Like her snapshots, her story focuses on and reveals the details of a woman's everyday life. Doris warns me she will talk forever if I give her the chance.

Doris becomes the grandmother I wish I'd had. She becomes the storyteller, comfortable telling her history, skilled in storytelling. If I'd had a grandmother like her, perhaps telling a story would come easier to me. It is easier to tell your stories to a stranger than to your own daughter, laughs Doris. Sitting at Doris's dining-room table, talking with her, looking at her photographs of family and friends, I begin to feel as if I am in the same "space" as the figures in her snapshots. I am no longer an observer looking back at events that happened long ago through photographs; I am there. Doris's stories transport my imagination, not just my eyes.

WRITING ON THE ROCKS

When I first walked up the stairs to her porch that morning, Doris asked me what I thought of the single red post outside her front door. I had noticed how it contrasted with the white walls and blue-painted porch. Without waiting for my answer, she started a story. Her sister had saved a post from the porch in front of their childhood home in Sweetwater. A nephew had brought it here to Cascade Locks. For years Doris kept it in a garage until they built a new home. Then she asked the builder to stick the post in somewhere. He asked her what color she wanted it painted. "I don't care what color it is, just so it's red," she replied. She was half-kidding, and the builder laughed, but he painted it red and found a way to build it into her new front porch.

Doris and mother

We settle back in our chairs at the dining-room table. Doris lifts another snapshot out of the basket. There is the post outside her Sweetwater home on one side of a flight of steps. On the other side is her mother. It is obviously summer. Flowers are blooming, and the sun is high and bright. Mama is a large woman, dressed in a long white skirt and short-sleeved shirt. She stands with her back to the wall of the Sweetwater house, firmly planted on the top of the porch steps. Maybe this is where Doris got her rooted look. The mother smiles down at Doris who must be about two years old. Dressed in a dark Red Cross outfit, Doris stares at the camera from beside the post. In this tiny brown-and-white photo, the post is white like the rest of the frame house, not the red column that graces her front porch today.

Scrutinizing the picture, I realize that most of my mental library of photographic images of American history are of men, exploring the nineteenth-century West, fighting in the Civil War, or standing in unemployment lines during the Depression. This is a picture of a woman, her child, and their domain, the house where they spend their days and nights. Because women remained home with their children and extended family, professional photographers did not often take their pictures, except in the studio. Home was a personal space, and women's lives were seen as too ordinary to merit examination. Their struggles were private ones and for the most part, unrecorded.

Doris and mother

Doris does not know who took the photograph she holds, but I suspect it was taken by a woman. The advent of small, affordable snapshot cameras gave women a special opportunity and new visibility. For the first time in photographic history, they did not need to become professionals or even serious hobbyists. They did not need substantial resources or time. They could photograph without needing an assistant to help carry and maneuver a bulky studio camera, and they no longer needed darkroom facilities for developing and printing. Immediately women, like Doris's sister, used the small cameras to record what they knew best—their families, their friends and their home life. I look at this tiny photo and wish I could hear Doris's mother's voice telling me what chores she was doing that morning, the worries she had about paying for the new shoes Doris needed and how she expected visitors for lunch.

Doris remembers those early days just as sharply as more recent ones. The post is enough to release a flood of memories, joining her Sweetwater childhood home to the present one in Cascade Locks. Between them is the mud dugout in Pie Town, New Mexico, where she and Faro raised Josie.

Everything leading up or back to it is chronological, but Pie Town is timeless. It lies somewhere between aspiration and memory—the way small American towns once did and still do in our literature. Life in such places is not something to remember or to wait for but just to live. For Doris, if she thought ahead at all in those days, it was to worry about whether she could still grow more cabbage plants to replace the ones the cow ate that morning. It was a time when she was so busy just living that she could not worry about the future.

Homesteading was something "off the grid," a tough life where bare essentials were all that mattered because they were all one had. It was not a better life but an unconventional one that resolute people like Doris took part in and embraced. To move to Divide, they gave up all that was comfortable and familiar. Yet the homesteading years of arduous labor without amenities or safety nets were more than a difficult time. They were a time rich in values, self-sufficiency, of "living in the moment." For Doris, her years in Pie Town between her childhood in Sweetwater and her more conventional later experiences are the strongest memories of her life. "We were dirt poor but didn't know it. We were happy and made our own fun." They were the period of her life that she experienced most intensely.

Doris at family home

Doris rummages in the basket and lifts out her daughter's first-grade report card.

> *I was just showing these to Josie a few days ago . . . pictures of her first school and stuff that wasn't in any of the photos that Lee made. Lee came to our house and he stayed with us. I told him that this was going on, and that was going on, and all this was south of Pie Town. All those that he made north of Pie Town and in Pie Town was people that came in later. We were the homesteaders.*

Doris likes the word "homesteader" and uses it in different ways throughout our conversations. She is proud of her association and wants to make sure I recognize the difference between those who filed and proved up on a claim and those who followed and bought relinquishments or finished what others had started. She was part of the first group, and she values that extra dirt under her fingernails.

Doris was part of a steady stream of hopeful and desperate Anglo immigrants who had pushed west ever since the 1862 Homestead Act. In New Mexico where most of the available land was rocky and high, only a trickle came at first. By the mid '20s and early '30s, as the Depression set in and work became too hard to find in other parts of the country, the trickle increased to a steady flow.

The homesteading story began long before Doris arrived. In the early nineteenth century, the plateau land of western New Mexico was home to the Zuni, who hunted and gathered throughout the territory. Trails to their sacred Salt Lake, located about forty miles northwest of Pie Town, were also used by the Laguna, Acoma, Hopi, and Navajos to gather salt. In the 1870s, Hispano homesteaders from central New Mexico began to push south and to establish a few small villages such as Quemado, Mangus, and Atarque near springs and rivers on the Zuni Plateau. The Hispano settlers, along with a few Anglos, formed a sparse base of settlement thinly spread in the region; they raised stock, engaged in subsistence agriculture, and maintained generally good relations with their Indian neighbors. Although to most early Anglo homesteaders like Doris, the land looked uninhabited and ready for the benefits of civilization, the reality was quite different.

Agnes Morley Cleaveland, a long-time rancher who lived twenty miles down the road from Pie Town in the Datil area, describes the scene in those early years:

> *I watched the homesteaders as they trekked by. They came in family groups, in any sort of conveyance that would roll, their household furnishings piled high and the overflow—washtubs, baby buggies, chicken coops—wired to any anchorage that would hold. In trucks, in automobiles, dragging heavy trailers, the rare exception in horse-drawn wagons, they came, and with them a new order. . . . Their clearings may be seen with the stumps of the pinyons still showing, or the dust of their plowed fields blowing across the face of the sky. A windmill is a rare exception, but "dirt tanks" for restraining floodwater during the rainy season are adjuncts of many of them.[5]*

Most of the homesteaders Cleaveland saw were "Texies," West Texans from the Panhandle and southern plains. Often a few family members, the bravest or the most desperate, left Texas, built a small dugout, and then encouraged others: "Come on out!" Mrs. L. M. Bolton's aunt and uncle wrote back to her in Lamesa, Texas, "This is a poor man's country. You can get started here." So she "drifted down into Pie Town," married a farmer and settled.[6]

For many who came during the Dust Bowl years, Pie Town was intended only as a stopover on the way to California. Mrs. Lewis West with her father and mother headed west on U.S. 60 in 1935. Five of their chickens suffocated in the Texas dust the morning they left. On their first night in Pie Town, ten more chickens died of the mountain cold. Her father was ill with heart trouble, so he and his wife and five children settled into a half-dugout and began to raise pinto beans and maize for cornmeal.[7]

For hopeful immigrants from the choking Dustbowl areas of Texas and Oklahoma, the reality of homesteading on the Zuni Plateau failed to live up to their dreams. The Pie Town area was unpromising for farming. The mountains were wooded, and the rolling valleys were covered with thick rabbitbrush, or *chamisa*, that made hand-clearing the land a tedious and back-breaking job. The growing season was usually too short with light frosts in early June and again in mid-September. Moisture was unreliable. Some years, when there was enough rain and snow, homesteaders might grow fine vegetable gardens and enough pinto beans or corn to sell for the necessities they could not grow themselves. Other years, the moisture was inadequate, and the rabbits, elk, or grasshoppers ate most of what was planted. Many homesteaders gave up and moved on to the cities where they joined unemployment lines. By the 1940s, when Russell Lee arrived to take his photographs for the FSA, the community had already declined from its 1935 peak to about two hundred families.

Doris succeeded in ways that transcended the hardships and outward appearances of failure. Yet she shakes her head when I ask her about the hard times. It was the living that mattered, not how hard she had to work. She had come from a family of homesteaders and had not expected anything else. Not everyone could do this. It was not enough to be resolute. It was not enough to be able to embrace the homesteading experience, to put in the time and the hard work; it seems you had to have a spark of innocence or naïveté that allowed you to go on hoping. You had to forget that you were "dirt poor," and you had to be capable of "making your own fun."

I once photographed an unmarked site in the Mojave Desert of California. It was little more than a jumbled pile of granite boulders much like other rocky hills in a rugged area of wind, stars, and Joshua trees. In the 1920s, a disgruntled John Samuelson built a small cabin and homesteaded at the base of the outcropping. He was a hardworking man who prospected a small mine nearby and hauled his water daily. Over a period of months Samuelson chiseled his anger on to the rock faces: "The milk of human kindness ain't got thick cream on it for all of us. Ask Hoover." He was bitter and railed against the economic system that made his life so difficult. Unlike Doris, Samuelson expected more.

Samuelson needed to write on the rocks. He wanted to tell others of his difficulties. He carved his legacy, cutting deep so that the letters would be as abiding as the rocks themselves. Lee, too, wanted to document what he saw. He once said of his work: "Well, I'm taking pictures of the history of tomorrow." Doris needs to talk about her pictures and the red post. Doris's legacy lives in a different way from Samuelson's—carved in stone—or Lee's, manifest in his photographs. Her legacy is in the snapshots taken by her family and friends and in her own words and stories that accompany and illuminate those images. Doris tells me she cannot spell so she is counting on me to tell her story in images and words for her grandchildren. What is important is to tell the story.

NOTHING BUT FUN

By 1935, the government had removed most "free" land from homesteading. Still, the searchers and strugglers continued to arrive. Instead of "proving up" on free land and fulfilling the requirements the government imposed for obtaining title, they bought cheap relinquishments from the Pie Town homesteaders who had already patented their lands but had given up homesteading and wanted to leave. By buying a relinquishment, they were buying the previous homesteader's right to "prove up" on a specific section of land that had already been listed in the county records as homestead acreage.

Roy McKee
Photo: Joan Myers

Not everyone failed. One of the later arrivals at Pie Town was Roy McKee, who took root and is there still. He and his brothers James and John came to Pie Town in 1937 from O'Donnell, Texas, and bought a relinquishment on 320 acres. Doris remembers him as a friend who came by every so often to visit. Today, he still lives in the log cabin that he built just southwest of town with his wife Maudie Bell, now deceased, and their oldest children.

On the summer day in 1995 when I visited him, we chatted on his front porch. Maudie Bell died in 1991, and Roy was living alone. Tall and rangy, only slightly stooped and bent at the knees with the weight of his eighty-five years, he is the spitting image of a western cowboy. He wore a stained black Stetson, dusty Levi's, and a long-sleeved denim shirt. His teeth, irregular but still adequate, outlined a long smile. As we talked he pulled a very large pocketknife with a white bone handle out of his pocket, flicked it open and trimmed his nails, one after the other, into perfect moonshapes. The double porch swing was made from an automobile front seat, and the way Roy smiled at me, showing a boyish pleasure in a woman's company, we might have been sixteen and out for a Sunday ride.

Roy and his family came to Pie Town from the south plains of west Texas in a car that they traded for Louis Johnson's relinquishment on a half section a few miles west of Pie Town. Along with the relinquishment, they also got a team of horses and a dozen chickens. Roy drove out from Texas in a tractor, pulling a sixteen-foot trailer-wagon built on car axles. The trip took ten days on the poor roads:

> It wasn't easy. Most of the way, it was just a couple of ruts, like a wagon road. Everywhere you looked, there was somebody broke down. Okies. Dusted out like us.
>
> I had everything we had—which wasn't much—in that trailer. The tractor ran on gas and coal oil and it didn't have any lights so I just stopped and camped at night.
>
> I came here for lots of reasons. I was ready to try anything after bucking those sandstorms. There was a bunch of us boys. You were doing good if you could find something to eat anywhere. You couldn't get a job. Nobody had anything for you to do. Everybody was just alike. Nobody had any money. You worked for $1.50 a day, hard work. If you didn't want to do it, somebody else was ready to go to work. Course the dollar was worth a lot more then than it is now.[8]

Today, Roy still manages to plant a huge garden, neat rows of corn, tomatoes, squash, beans, and cabbage. He could move in with one of his children who left Pie Town long ago, but he has no plans to do that. At his age, he told me, he does not have any plans. He offers me a sackful of the most enormous squash I have ever seen to take with me from his "little acre of garden down there" and tells me:

> I just have to work that garden to keep from going crazier than what I already am. I just got to have something to do. I'm getting so I can't put out much work. I've been here about sixty years. It still looks all right to me, but I ain't going to see her much longer, am I?

I'm not too good. Ain't nothing wrong with me. Just had too many birthdays. That'll do it.

Roy remembers Doris. "Old Doris. For Heaven's sake. It has been many moons since I seen her. I'd like to see her. Doris and Faro. Yeah, I knew them real well. Old Faro, he was like everybody else. He had to work to make a living up there."

Like Roy McKee, Doris grew up poor. Born 28 September 1915, she was the youngest of her siblings in a family of homesteaders in Sweetwater, Texas. Her mother Bertha was only fourteen when she married Doris's father George Warner Altizer in 1898 in Cherokee, Texas. He was seventeen and earning a living breaking wild horses for ranches in the area. Doris shows me a photograph of herself as a toddler with her dad in front of that homestead in Sweetwater and tells me there was nothing with four feet that her dad could not ride.

When he found a job working horses on the Seals's ranch in Hilton, Texas, the family loaded all their possessions in a borrowed wagon and team and moved them to Hilton. Doris remembers that it took several days to make the trip and that they did not have a cent to their name. One day her mother found a dime shining half-buried in the wagon ruts and thought it was the most money she had ever seen.

After he finished breaking all the horses on the ranch, her dad got a steady job carrying the mail horseback from Hilton to Sweetwater and back the next day. He was paid $1.00 per trip.

Then, my folks moved to Sweetwater and rented a place up on the hill about where the end of the overpass going west is now. Then Dad bought a city block there on Walnut Street. He was a house-moving contractor by then. There was a little house at the Santa Fe depot that they weren't using so they sold it to Dad. He moved it on to this block. Dad and Mama lived in it until they got their house built. They built two rooms first and then three rooms and then a great big hall down the middle of it. They built it piecemeal, as they could.

I was born in Sweetwater, Texas, in this house I'm talking about.

I was the baby of the family. I've got a list of all the kids I can send you. You know, I'm the last living of our litter. That's real hard.

Doris was born sixteen years after her parents' marriage, the last of the five children who survived childhood. Now all but Doris are gone. So many have died, she tells me. Her life was so different from her daughter's, her granddaughter's or her great-granddaughter's. She wants them to know the difference before she, too, is gone.

Doris's grandfather at Cherokee

When Doris was a kid, she dreamed of going to Alaska. She read stories about the dog teams and the snow and the Northern Lights. She imagined herself living with Eskimos in an igloo, seeing wolves, and hunting seals. But Doris's options were tied to those she lived with: her parents first, and then her husband, whenever she married. She knew she would find a way to fashion her own life but she did not know how. Her tale is a woman's tale of moving west in pursuit of a patented dream of a better life. But the patent has always belonged to men; they, after all, had the freedom and resources to set out for unknown territory. Homesteading for her was a woman's way of making good on her dreams.

For Doris, it was unthinkable that a woman without a husband might make a life of her own in a different part of the country. A woman's life decisions were contingent on her husband's. She could not just take off to look for work in another part of the country. How was she to do it? Even the idea would not have occurred to her, much less a plan of action. Instead, she sent her dreams as scouts to go before her.

Her opportunity came in 1929 when she was just fourteen.

When I was in high school, my best girl friend was Neely Jo Mickey. We became lifelong friends, and we still write to each other. She was three years older than I and the daughter of our Church of Christ minister there in Sweetwater, George F. Mickey. You see, Brother Mickey's mother, Sally Mickey, and her sister, Julia Mickey, and seven of his cousins all homesteaded eleven miles south of Pie Town, New Mexico, at the foot of Alegra Mountain. Since Sally and Julia married Mickey brothers, their children were really double cousins, because they were kin on both sides.

There was no church at that time out there anywhere, so George Mickey's mother wrote to him and asked if he would come out and hold meetings at the different schoolhouses. He arranged to spend about two months each summer for the next three years holding weeklong meetings at the different school houses. One cousin lived at Dove Creek, Colorado, so we went up there, too.

The Mickeys invited me to go along on this trip because Jo needed a companion, and my mother said I could go. Mother and Dad knew Brother and Sister Mickey and Neely Jo real well. I was almost fifteen, and Jo was three years older than I was.

Doris does not remember how long it took to get from Sweetwater to Pie Town. What she does remember is her excitement. Back home in Sweetwater she already had boyfriends and invitations to parties, but she did not hesitate when her parents said she could go.

I remember that we went by Elephant Butte Dam and the old Hot Springs. Now it's called Truth or Consequences. We spent the night and Brother Mickey preached there. Then we went out to Elephant Butte. There were lots of things like that I got to see. We went to Las Cruces and stayed there for about four days, I guess. We got to see everything around. We went by Alamogordo and saw the white sands. Of course that was a hundred years before the atomic blast. I saw a lot of things that, had I not gone with them, I would never have seen.

We had nothing but fun. We counted the windmills, Neely Jo and I. The first one to see a windmill . . . we got a little notebook,

and the first time we saw a windmill we'd put our mark on that.
We'd see who could find the most. Every time we found a white
horse, we would snap our fingers and put it in our palm and make
a wish and knew that wish would come true because we had found
this white horse. Just silly stuff like that.

The Mickeys and Doris traveled in a touring car with two seats, and most of the time she and Neely Jo slept in the car at night. Most of the other roads were dirt or gravel and very narrow. Brother Mickey would drive for a couple of days, hold a meeting, and then go on for a couple of nights some place else. Gradually they worked their way west to Pie Town and the Mickey homesteads. It was not an easy trip. The last stretch, from Socorro through Magdalena and Datil to Pie Town, was an especially rough segment of Highway 60 with deep ruts on the steep hills.

When Doris arrived in Pie Town, she found a small, isolated community. The daily stage (an automobile fitted with roof and fender racks) was the primary contact with the outside world, bringing newspapers, mail, and supplies for the general store as well as passengers reluctant to drive through the sparsely populated region. On the north side of the dirt highway was a small hotel with a sign that said Pie Town. The bean house, the taxidermy store, and the church that Lee photographed came later.

On the opposite side of the street, down the hill, was the general store run by Harmon Craig. Behind the store was a big grove of trees. Doris tells me that whenever anybody from Divide came into town, they would park out there because they could not afford to license their cars, and if the state police came by they would not see the unlicensed car. There was no doctor, no electricity, no telephone, and no running water.

Water, scarce even at the town pump, was only used for essential tasks, and often reused. In the hotel with the Pie Town sign, where Russell and Jean Lee later stayed, there was no shower or bath. The Lees remembered going outdoors to pump water for a bath. They carried it indoors in a bucket and heated it on the wood stove in the hotel lobby. Then they poured the hot water into a large metal tub. Lee probably decided not to process any test film during their stay since he would have had to carry all the water that he used in his makeshift darkroom by hand. Although the Lees had all the water they needed during their stay, in dry periods the town water supply often ran out entirely.

Even today, in Cascade Locks, where water drips from the window frames for days on end, Doris still loves being able to get running water from a sink tap. She cannot forget the time in Pie Town when most people did not even have well water of their own and had to haul what they needed. She remembers that just inside the doorway of the Pie Town store, store owner Craig kept a bucket of water and a dipper so that anyone who came in could get a drink. Doris can still recall the warm mineral taste of it that June day when she and the Mickeys first drove into Pie Town.

The Mickeys at Divide

One of Lee's photos shows the doorway of this Pie Town store. The store was made from local materials, the chairs, shelving, and cafe counter from split logs; the pie cabinet was just shelves with screen wire to keep the flies off. Mr. Keele, president of the Farm Bureau and, by 1940, co-owner of the store with Harmon Craig, carries a box of groceries out of the store, standing in the doorway on pine boards that have curled and warped in the dry air and high-altitude sun. Around him, nailed about the wide doorway, is advertising for Beech-Nut and Union Standard chewing tobacco, for Golden Grain, Kool, and Avalon cigarettes and a poster for horse races in Magdalena. Hand-lettered signs give the mileage from Pie Town to points east and west.

Pie Town was known simply as "Norman's Place" at first. Clyde Norman was an ex-serviceman who came to New Mexico at the end of the First World War, hoping to homestead. In October 1922, when he could not find a claim he liked, he filed a Mining Location

Notice for the Hound Pup Lode, a forty-acre piece of property near what later became known as the transcontinental Highway 60. To subsidize his mining operation, he started buying gasoline, kerosene, and grocery items some seventy-five miles away, in Magdalena. He then resold them at the one-room picket house with a sign that read: "NORMAN'S PLACE. Gas and Oil for Sale—Free water for Radiators."

Norman knew that cowboys, sheep herders, and other travelers passing through on the east-west highway also needed something to eat, so he started selling coffee with doughnuts that he bought from Helen McLaughlin's bakery in Datil. When she found he was reselling them, she told him to make his own. But his were not very good, so he switched to pie making. He liked to bake his pies with dried apples, using a recipe he learned as a teenager in Texas. They were an immediate success. Soon after, he replaced his original sign with a hand-stenciled one that said: "Pie Town."

Two years later, a redheaded Texas cowboy from Jacksboro named Harmon L. Craig bought a working interest in Pie Town and started adding other baked products and a zippy chili-con-carne. Eventually, Craig bought out Norman's half-ownership, and he and his new wife, Theora, and her two daughters from a previous marriage ran the store and café for many years. "Out of pure hellishness," he successfully battled the federal government to have the town called Pie Town. Craig then succeeded in getting his store declared a United States post office and became its first postmaster. Pie Town was official.

In 1933, Joe A. Keele, the man carrying the boxes in Lee's photograph of the Pie Town store, and his wife Carrie, left Texas with the knowledge that it could not get any worse than where they had been. They arrived in Pie Town with six cents to their name and homesteaded for several years. Carrie taught school, and Joe did carpentry for Harmon Craig. Eventually, he became Craig's partner in the Craig and Keele General Merchandise Store.

I show Doris one of Lee's photographs of Harmon Craig. He is dressed in a dirty white shirt, denim overalls, and a white Sherwin Williams Paint paper hat. He has his eyes closed and is sitting on sacks of pinto beans that fill the frame behind him. The photo caption says, "Mr. Craig allows local farmers to store surplus beans in his warehouse free of charge. He also makes them interest-free loans."

Doris laughs.

I hate to say this, but that old buzzard never gave anybody anything. He demanded blood. He married a lady and she had two girls, and she was real nice.

When Craig took over the store from Norman, he put in gas pumps and enlarged the inventory. Craig offered advice to new farmers, permitted them to charge their groceries for the entire year until harvest time, loaned cash, and bought and sold land for homesteaders. His wife and daughters cooked for the café, baking up to fifty cherry, raisin, or apple pies a day, pies "like mother used to make." They also helped customers with gas and oil and with store goods. Years later, Theodora said of him, "He cussed a lot, but he cussed nice clean cussing."[9]

When I ask Doris if she ever bought pies at Craig's café, she laughs because she and Faro did not have money for stamps or toilet paper, much less to buy pies from the café. She did bake pies, though. They grew pinto beans, so once in a while she would make a bean pie. It was not bad, she says; tasted a lot like pumpkin. They did not have any berries or fresh fruit, but sometimes she could trade vegetables or a chicken for dried fruit and then make fruit pies. At Christmas time only, she would make a coconut cream pie. Faro loved chocolate pies best, and when she could afford a little sugar and cocoa she would make him a chocolate pie to put him in a good mood.

She talks about once going to a dance ten miles away, at the Biggers place, south of the mountain. Walking or riding on horseback were their only means of transportation, so she rode Faro's trusty Blue Dog, while Faro rode a young mare he was breaking. Doris made a chocolate pie for the dance, and as they rode along Faro carried the pie until they got to a gate; then he would hand it to her and get down and open the gate. There were twenty-three gates on that journey. By the time they arrived, she jokes, the pie had racked up the equivalent of one hundred thousand frequent flier miles.

"What times we had!"

She picks another photograph out of the basket, blows the dust off it and, like a genie, culls a story out of the image. It is an image of her leaning against a log building, tiny and slightly out of focus. This building was on the Mickey homestead where Brother Mickey's relatives lived. Excitedly, she tells me how they found their way from Pie Town to the homesteading community of Divide where the Mickeys lived.

> Brother Mickey went in to the store and asked Mr. Craig how to get to the home of Burley Mickey. Faro's Dad, "Pop" Caudill, was standing there and he heard him. He said, "I live on the place right next to Burley, and if you'll follow me home, I'll take you right there."
>
> So we followed Pop. As we were driving out we kept seeing this one real tall mountain sitting off to itself. We later learned it was called "Old Legra"—Alegra Mountain, really, but Old Legra was what everyone called it. Pop and Lizzie, his wife, had an old Model A touring car with a piece of oilcloth pasted up on the roof to keep it from leaking. Their son Faro's dog, Old Pat, rode out on the hood of the car everywhere they went. So when we got to the turnoff, they said, "Now, Burley lives the next place over."

The Burley Mickey homestead was located some eleven miles south of the Pie Town store and post office in a homesteading community on the skirts of Alegra Mountain. The community called itself Divide, since it straddled the Continental Divide, but it was not an official town and had no post office or commercial buildings. It was made up of the Mickey cousins and their families and just a few other families. The Mickey homestead had been cleared of most of the ponderosa pine that forested the mountain and its immediate vicinity, and the small log structures that Doris saw as she drove in appeared lost in the wide scrubby landscape. Compared to her modest but comfortable home in Sweetwater, the buildings looked primitive and isolated.

The log house in the photograph Doris shows me is where she and Neely Jo stayed that first summer they came to Divide. The rough wood building adjoined the Burley Mickey house and was nothing more than a lean-to with a bed in it. The photo shows Doris standing behind Neely Jo with her arm on Neely Jo's shoulder. Neely Jo sits on a log stump with a tin washtub and other household implements hanging on the wall behind her. Both girls wear sleeveless dresses and have the awkward prettiness of young teenage girls.

Seeing this image reminds me of the snapshot that Doris showed me of their arrival in Pie Town. After they stopped in the store to ask directions to Burley Mickey's place in Divide, she and Neely Jo each walked up to the hotel, the same hotel where Russell Lee and his wife would later stay, and posed so that Sister Mickey could take their picture under the Pie Town sign.

> *We both had on what I think in those days they called "lounging pajamas." They were stylish at that time for girls to wear, and Jo and I both had on a pair. Pop Caudill walked out of the store and saw us, and he put his hands on his hips and said, "Now ain't that a hell of a garb for a preacher's kids to be wearing." You know they just didn't wear things like that. It was such a garb for us to have on. You don't remember back then, but when women first started to wear pants, they didn't wear jeans. They wore these big-legged long pajamas. Isn't that something?*

Of course she was not a preacher's kid, but Fred Caudill's comment about her "lounging pajamas" tickled her enough that she remembers it vividly sixty-five years later. Sister Mickey's picture shows Doris at fourteen, on her first trip away from home, delighted with herself and eager for whatever adventure lay ahead. Today, sitting at her table in Cascade Locks, Oregon, she giggles like a teenager at that picture because it reminds her of how she felt then, standing outside the Pie Town store.

THAT TALL ONE IS MINE

After Pop Caudill pointed out the turnoff to Burley Mickey's house, Brother Mickey thanked him. He encouraged Faro to come to church that night for the service he would preach. The Mickeys in Divide shared a Church of Christ faith going back to their lives in Texas. Of course he would be there, Faro replied, although he was neither a Mickey nor a Church of Christ follower. He told Brother Mickey that the meeting had been the talk of the community for weeks.

That evening, when the Mickeys and Doris arrived at the Divide schoolhouse that served as the community church, homesteaders from the surrounding areas had already taken their seats. A few people had driven up in Model T Fords, but most had come by horseback, in wagons, or on foot. At seven-thirty on a warm summer night, it was not yet dark, but people had brought lamps and lanterns to light up the schoolhouse. There was no electricity closer than Magdalena, sixty miles away.

What happened that night is one of Doris's strongest memories. Even with no photo to prompt her, she remembers all the details.

> *Faro and Fatty Biggers weren't there that night because someone south of the mountain was having a dance so they had gone. The next morning Faro's dad told them the preacher had two good-looking daughters and they should have gone to meet them. He didn't know until later that I wasn't a preacher's daughter. So, they said, "OK, we'll go, hangover or not."*
>
> *The next night Faro and Fatty came to the meeting, and before they went into the schoolhouse they peeped into it to see if they could see the new girls. They could. Faro said, "That tall one is mine if I never get her." That was his comment about me. I was taller than Neely Jo. When I was young, my hair was dishwater blond and so fine that it broke off by the time it got to be shoulder length.*

In the sixty-five years since that night in Pie Town when she first met Faro, Doris has felt few other moments in her life so acutely. She does not tell me that directly, but I can hear the excitement in her voice. She shifts in her chair and entwines her fingers restlessly.

Doris and Neely Jo

The boys all came in a body and sat in the back seats. When Clarence and Oscar Schalbar came in, Mick Dees said to them, "Clarence and Oscar, come on up here. I want you to meet these two girls." She introduced Jo and I to them. Clarence was so shy that when they were introduced to us, he wheeled around and knocked off the lantern and broke it because he was in such a hurry to get away. If it hadn't been retrieved, he'd have set the whole place on fire!

Then Faro came up, and they introduced us. Faro just happened to sit by me. After church he asked me to go horseback riding with him, and I told him I would.

The next day after the horseback ride, Faro asked her to climb the mountain with him.

Alegra Mountain rises from about eight thousand feet at its base to ten thousand feet at the summit with dry rocky flanks. It was a long, hot, scrambling ascent. But as they climbed, Doris and Faro told stories, laughed, and got to know each other. When they eventually reached the flat summit, they found themselves at timberline. Far below they could see the openings in the trees that marked clearings for homestead dugouts and gardens and the school. A red-tailed hawk swooped downward in the indigo sky.

Amid the few stunted ponderosas near the summit, they found a fruit jar with a lid. Inside were the names of climbers who had come before them. Doris and Faro wrote their names on a scrap of paper and put it in the jar along with those of previous climbers. When she comes out to visit me, Doris says, we will climb to the top of Alegra Mountain and see if the names are still there.

Every day for a week Doris and Faro went somewhere together. In church at night, she tells me, they held hands under the songbook and smiled at each other.

One Sunday, Brother Mickey baptized Aunt Lizzie, Faro, Fatty, Clarence, and Oscar and several others. Because water was so scarce, and none was available at Divide, they decided to go to a dirt tank over on the plains and baptize everyone the same day.

After the baptizing, Pop donated a cow for a barbecue. He butchered it, and the men dug a great big long pit and barbecued the whole cow. They made their own sauce.

The ladies all brought things to go with it like cakes and pies, and we had a big dinner on the ground with everyone invited. I didn't do too much besides make goo-goo eyes at all the boys. It sure was good!

Doris and Neely Jo at Divide school

After that week, Brother Mickey then toured the area's small communities, preaching for a week or so in the schoolhouse in each town. Young women were not frequent visitors to the remote homestead areas, and all the young boys catered to Doris and Neely Jo. Often, local communities threw parties in honor of the preacher's visit. She remembers doing a lot of laughing and flirting. For Doris, traveling with the Mickeys as a "preacher's kid" was a respectable way to have fun and she made the most of it.

Doris confides to me that she continued to see Faro even after leaving Divide and that a team of plow horses had given them away:

When the Mickeys left there, we went to Green's Gap south of the mountain for the next week, and Faro came down there and spent the week with Fatty Biggers. The next week we were going to Mountain View, a community about twenty miles north of Pie Town. The second night we were there, who should appear but Faro and Fatty Biggers.

Faro was plowing, and Fatty came by and asked him if he wanted to go to Mountain View, and Faro left the team hitched to the plow in the middle of the field and took off. When Pop came home from somewhere and found the team and no Faro, he couldn't imagine where he was or why he had left the team in the field all

hooked up. When Faro did get home about a week later Pop sure had
plenty to say to him.

When we finally left all the communities around Pie Town where
Brother Mickey had been preaching, Pop was really glad. He said,
"Now I can get some work out of that boy again."

When Doris returned home after that first summer away, she
saw her family life with a new perspective. The trip had given her
a bird's eye view of the life she had grown up in. Familiar routines
had shrunk to small outcroppings in a much larger landscape. Her
primary chore at home was to chop wood by the hour. Her family
used wood for everything, both heating and cooking. All the time
she chopped she thought of the towns she had stopped in and the
people she had met. She looked out the window of her bedroom at
familiar terrain—the house across the street where the woman lived
who had nine kids and beyond that the open land with mesquite
trees that the Sweetwater outskirts bled into. And, hardly trying, Doris
also saw Alegra Mountain and the dugouts, heard the calls of the
coyotes, and smelled the sage and the afternoon rainsqualls that mainly
evaporated before reaching the dry ground.

For Doris, Sweetwater dwindled in importance even as she
continued to mark time living there. As she did her schoolwork,
she remembered the long car journey with Neely Jo and the Mickeys.
Her dreams had scouted out the journey and now her memories
revisited it.

Mostly she thought of Faro and their climb up Alegra Mountain.
Sitting, holding hands, talking. Faro telling her she was the prettiest
girl around. Doris wanted to see him again. Their letters to each
other carried them through the long winter and spring. She could
hardly wait for summer when, once again, she accompanied the
Mickeys west to Pie Town.

Other boys liked her, too, but Faro's big nose and appetite made
him and Doris a pair.

I liked Faro. Oscar and Clarence and, well, all of the boys . . . I could
have gone with any of them. In fact, this Dave Shough ran a garage
where he fixed cars over at Pie Town, and he wrote to me for a

while. Oscar wrote to me for a while and several of the boys, and they all asked me for dates, but I liked Faro better than the rest of them, so I went with Faro. I don't know what I liked about him. He was real nice. He had a great big nose, and he and I both liked to eat. Frank Dees, the one-armed guy who was married to Mick Dees who was a Mickey and a nurse in the war, they used to kid us and say if we ever got married our kids would have the longest noses in the world and we couldn't see them because we were such big eaters. We didn't care.

Doris lifts Faro Caudill out of the basket. It is a snapshot taken in their homestead corral, part of which had a narrow roof made of peeled logs to provide shade for the animals. Faro, his broad-brimmed hat shading all of his face but the tip of his nose and chin, is squatting on the ground just in front of the shaded area. He has his arm around a tiny white calf.

After the second summer, when we got ready to go home, the last night we were there, Faro asked me to marry him and I told him I would. Then we still wrote, and I still didn't tell my parents or anybody. The only person that knew that he had asked me to marry him was Neely Jo. We just courted for those three years that I went out there. We were a thing.

Russell Lee also photographed Faro. He is squatting on the ground as he is in Doris's snapshot, but this time he is rolling a cigarette and telling stories to his neighbors. Other Lee images show him dismantling the logs, digging out a new floor, and moving his dugout to a new location. Another has him watching Doris cooking dinner over a campfire while the dugout is being rebuilt.

Doris shows me yet another Lee image, this time in color, which she has carefully saved in the basket with her family snapshots. It is from a 1979 issue of *Modern Photography* and is a photograph made with the new color transparency material that Roy Stryker, head of the Historical Division of the Farm Security Administration sent Lee to experiment with.[10] In a take-off on Grant Wood's *American Gothic*, Faro in a work-stained shirt stands next to Doris in front of a picket fence. Doris's arms are crossed. Faro stands shoulder to shoulder with her, slightly shorter, even with his Indiana Jones hat. Faro is a handsome man, dark complexioned and with the shadow of a day-old beard. There is a cigarette wedged in the corner of his mouth. His chewed-up felt hat hides his eyes but not his wide ears. You sense his unruffled nature, so easy that even his sister Loraine says she never saw him get angry.

Faro and Doris stand close, their arms touching, their slight smiles there for the photographer. Of the two, Doris appears the more solidly planted. Lee has shot them from a low angle so they stand with their heads outlined against a blue sky. They are as much a part of the land and sky as the clouds that hang above them, and you get the sense that even though this land is hard on people, it is also their lifeblood.

Faro and his younger sister Loraine had moved to New Mexico from Missouri in 1927 with their father Fred Caudill and their Aunt Lizzie Schalbar. Faro's grandfather had migrated from Spain to North Carolina, and then further west. At some point their Spanish name, Caudillo, was Anglicized to Caudill and sometimes spelled Cordell or Cordle. Doris says Faro and his father always pronounced the name with the accent on the first syllable, *Cau'dill*.

The story around Pie Town today is that Faro's father Fred and his Uncle Oscar came from Oklahoma and moved into Texas where they began stealing stock. They would change a brand slightly and claim it as their own. When they were run out of Texas, they decided to homestead in New Mexico.

Doris tells it more circumspectly:

As far as Pop and his brother Oscar being cattle rustlers or any-thing like that, there's nothing to that tale. They were renegades, but that's how renegades were. You know what I mean. They didn't do anything like thieving and stealing cattle and all that . . . well, I guess they might rustle a few cattle in the winter if they needed food, but . . . mainly they told a lot of tall tales.

Oscar and Fred worked on the L/Z Ranch in Texas, one of the biggest ranches in Texas, as cattle drivers. They traveled to Kansas

City with the cattle, and on one of those trips Fred met a young French immigrant named Josie and married her. Doris's daughter Josie is named for this grandmother whom she never knew. After they married, Fred and his wife lived in Loraine, Texas. Faro was born there, followed by Loraine, Faro's sister.

When Faro's mother died of cancer several years later, Pop wrote to her sister, Aunt Lizzie, who was living in Missouri, near Springfield, and told her that Josie had passed away. Lizzie Schalbar was already a widow when Josie died. She and Fred continued to correspond, and when Fred went out to visit Lizzie in Missouri, they decided to get married. Thus, Lizzie became Faro's stepmother as well as being his aunt. Fred needed a mother for his children and Lizzie wanted a father to help her bring up her small children.

Doris tells me that Uncle Oscar was the first member of the family to move to the Pie Town area. He married a woman half his age named Huldy. They had some thirteen kids, and named the boys and girls alike, every one of them, Oscar—Oscar Star, Oscar Lewis, Oscar Roscoe, and Oscar Babe. That way they could always count on one of them coming to help if they called out, "Oscar."

When Lizzie and Fred decided to join Oscar and Huldy, Lizzie also brought her two sons with her, Clarence and Oscar Schalbar. The family arrived in two new Model T Ford touring cars and shipped their cattle, horses, and mules on the train to Magdalena. They lived for a couple of months in a cabin on Oscar's place near Quemado before starting to homestead out at Alegra Mountain.

The marriage of convenience between Fred and Lizzie was not a happy one and lasted less than a year. When they separated she kept the original place, still known in the area as the Schalbar place, and lived there with her two sons. Fred and his two kids moved about a mile and a half away into a house and half-dugout that had been built by a previous homesteader but not proved up on.

Homesteading life was difficult enough for a family working together. For a single man like Fred with two children, alcohol became an easily available coping mechanism for too much work and uncomfortable responsibilities. Roy McKee has lived in Pie Town since 1937, and when I chatted with him out on his front porch, he remembered Fred as "bad to drink."

> *I knew old Fred well. He lived over there up on the mountain for years and years. He had one boy and a girl that lived there with him. They was pretty small. He couldn't stay off of that bottle. He stayed drunk, spent all the money he got for whiskey, and the kids like to starve to death, Loraine and Faro. She was still a kid. Faro was about grown when I come here in 1937, but he was a young-looking guy.*

Doris remembers Pop as a great storyteller who kept them rapt with his escapades on both sides of the law as they sat before an orange-tongued fireplace on winter evenings. Even when he was not directly involved, he seemed to have a way of knowing the most exciting gossip throughout the county. One such true story about neighboring rancher Henry Coleman was a lurid tale of rustling, adultery, and murder. Pop and his brother Oscar had both been involved in the case and indeed arrested for a short time, but no evidence was offered against them at the trial. Doris says they would shiver each time he got to the ending where a neighborhood posse armed with high-powered rifles gunned down both Coleman and his horse without giving them a chance for surrender.

Doris related what it was like for Faro and his sister Loraine before she got out there.

> *You see, Faro'd go off and work over north of Pie Town and come home every once in a while, and he'd bring his check over to Pop and Loraine for groceries and things. Pop wasn't working. Faro was just in and out. He didn't live there too much at home after they moved there because he was off working. He was young, yeah, sure he was young when we married but he grew up fast. He had to.*
>
> *It was hard for Loraine, real hard. One year Pop went off to Hot Springs and married another one of his wives. I kept Loraine and sent her to school and Faro went off to cut fence posts with Dick Fowler. Loraine was just a kid, but she and I took care of the stock.*

I ask Doris to back up and to tell me how she and Faro got married. Does she have any mementos?

I still have the original telegram that he wired me when he was coming down to get me, when we got married. He said: "Am coming. Have had some trouble. Love, Faro." You have to decode that any way you can. I didn't know when he was coming or the trouble he'd had or anything.

It was typical of Faro to send such a wry, enigmatic message, she tells me. His disposition amused all that knew him. Like his father, Faro was an entertainer—a stand-up comic, a singer who made up his own songs and an auctioneer when called upon. He loved to tell stories and always saw the best side of people. Doris knew she did not need to worry about the trouble Faro had and that one way or another he was coming to marry her.

She tells me that she and Faro decided during her third summer visit to Pie Town that they would get married back in Sweetwater as soon as she finished her final high-school year. During the summer of 1932 when Doris graduated, Faro was working for Frank Dees at the sawmill, hoping to have enough saved by Christmas to come after her. As it turned out, times were so hard that he could not get any cash for his work, just store credit that he used to buy tobacco and a little food from the mill commissary.

Fall came, then Christmas. Faro still had no transportation and no money. Finally, in desperation, he took a load of lumber to Magdalena and on the way stopped at Pine Park and traded his best cow to D. B. Williams to get a ride to Sweetwater. Williams brought his wife along with him. Clarence Schalbar also came along, hoping to marry Doris's friend Neely Jo. On February 7, 1933, Faro and Doris were married.

The night before they came was one of the coldest spells Sweetwater and West Texas had had in over fifty years. Faro and Dad went up to get the preacher, and the car froze on the way up. When they got back, the preacher, Brother Teddlie, ate dinner with us. As we were eating Faro started to cut some butter. It was so cold that the butter was frozen, and it sailed off the table and right into the preacher's lap. Everyone kidded Faro about being a nervous bridegroom.

After dinner we gathered in the front room. In the same house where I was born, I was married. Later my daughter Josie was born there. Mama died there in the same room.

The wedding was on a Tuesday, and by early Friday morning they started back to Pie Town. Neely Jo wanted to marry Clarence and come with them to Divide, but her father, Brother Mickey, objected. He was fond of his beautiful daughter and did not want her marrying a penniless homesteader. Even though Neely Jo was three years older than Doris, she did not oppose her father's wishes. Doris shakes her head over that. Neely Jo did marry a man of her father's liking soon after and had two children by him, but she didn't really love him, and they soon divorced. Clarence had come to Sweetwater with Faro, sweet dreams in his head and a ring in his pocket. When Neely Jo refused him, he was bitter and humiliated. The experience "cooked him on women" for the rest of his life. Although he did eventually marry, the marriage was not a satisfying one. His mother, Aunt Lizzie, never got over the rejection either. She kept her hand-embroidered tea towels "for Clarence and Neely Jo" in an old trunk until her death.

Doris laughs mischievously. She has never had trouble making decisions. Whether it is right or wrong, once she has made a decision, she has followed it. If her father had objected, she would have married Faro anyway, she says. Then she adds that I did not hear her say that.

So we left Sweetwater, Faro and I and Clarence and D. B. Williams and his wife. The weather was still bad—snow and ice everywhere and the snow was knee-deep. It took us about three nights on the road. We camped out in the snow. After we had made our bonfire and cooked our supper, we raked away the coals and made a big Methodist pallet on the warm ground and slept out. The men slept on the two outsides, and Mrs. Williams and I were in the middle. It sure was cold, but we all slept together and had lots of fun and didn't have a worry in the world.

PEPPERMINT DROPS

For all that know her, Doris behaves as if she is their only caretaker and always will be. No matter what I bring her when I come to visit, she always makes sure I leave with more than I brought. A beaded necklace, a hand-embroidered dishtowel, a jar of home-canned huckleberry jam. She is the same way with all her friends and family. She constantly worries about how best to help and give pleasure to everyone she knows, but in the midst of her energy and hard work she believes that some greater force is in charge.

> *I know that God will take care of us. He always has, and he always will.*
>
> *There's not a day when I say my prayers that I'm not thankful for the electricity we have, for being able to go to the tap for water instead of having to haul it so far, to be able to take a bath and have all the water I want. Those are the things homesteading taught me.*

When Doris arrived in Pie Town as a new bride, she was only seventeen. She had grown up the youngest in the family, with two sisters and two brothers, and was unaware of most of the family's economic struggles. She was accustomed to hard work but always within a busy household that nonetheless took the time to cater to her as the baby of the family.

> *My parents said I was spoiled rotten, but I don't think I was.*

Doris adored her father. Even with the uncertainty of his contract house-moving work and his need to travel frequently, he always had time for his family. One night he took Doris and her mother to hear a radio for the first time. They walked up to a small service station just up the road from them in Sweetwater, and there was a whole room of people waiting to listen to the magical new invention. You had to go up one at a time and put on earphones to hear it, she tells me, and the owner let each person listen for just a minute. When it was her turn she heard voices singing, "O, those golden slippers/O, those golden slippers/O, those golden slippers/ We're going to walk the golden streets."

How could you forget it?

Doris's mother Bertha, a large-boned woman with rosy cheeks and a beautiful complexion, was the lifeline of the family. She was fun-loving, enjoyed playing jokes on her friends and family, and Doris remembers her riding astride rather than sidesaddle. It was she who paid all the bills and made sure the family had enough to eat. Even though the family's income was always uncertain due to her father's lack of a salaried, dependable job, Doris felt comfortable inviting her friends home for dinner because the family always had plenty of food on the table. Every year her mother planted a big garden. In the summer they had corn, peas, beans, greens, tomatoes, and onions, which she also canned and dried for winter. In addition, her mother's cow guaranteed a good supply of fresh milk and butter, and her chickens provided fresh eggs and meat.

Strangers were welcome at the Altizer home. The family lived just a block from the railroad, and every tramp that rode the rails into Sweetwater made a beeline to their house. They always passed up the other houses on the block because Doris's mother was a joyful, hard-working woman and the best cook in the neighborhood. The iceman said he would rather have one of Mrs. Altizer's buttermilk biscuits than anyone else's cake.

Doris got her Christian faith from her mother. All the Altizers were members of the Church of Christ, and their faith was part of their upbringing. Doris says she still thinks of her mother when she walks into church and hears the old hymns like "The Old Rugged Cross" and "Count Your Many Blessings." She remembers the time when her parents took her to a meeting in the black part of town. They were the only white people there. Her dad put a five-dollar bill in the collection plate, and the man passing it said loudly, "Thank you, Mr. Altizer." Her mother laughed about it later and told Doris she thought the congregation was going to ask her dad to preach.

Doris hated to leave her parents and her Sweetwater home. She knew she was going several long days' drive away—so far that visits would be rare. She and Faro would have no telephone at the dugout. The nearest one was at the Forest Service office about sixty-five miles away in the hills on the outskirts of Magdalena. Even the touristy Navajo Lodge in Datil lacked a phone, so Doris could not even think about calling.

Doris felt so out of touch she might as well have been setting off for the Arctic Circle by dogsled. But, she confides, she did not have enough sense to be scared. When you are eighteen and in love, she says, you will do anything.

Doris must have been more excited than she now lets on. She says little to me about how she felt, just that she waited eagerly for Faro to come for her all the time he was working to save up enough money. All that time, she anticipated the marriage and the journey to Pie Town and planned her married life. She made quilts, embroidered towels, and bought a hope chest. There were moments in the day when she looked up from helping her mother wash clothes and realized her thoughts and heart had already left home on their journey west.

Doris's parents and grandparents

Most of Doris's friends married and stayed in Texas, surrounded by the family, friends, landscape, and furniture they had known all their lives. But Doris had a brave preference for life outside that loop. She does not see herself as brave, but I do. She did more than dream of setting out. She left behind all that she had known, not only her family and home but small, familiar objects like the piano in the front room, the wood box she was supposed to keep filled, the neighbor's dog that barked at cats, and Sweetwater's dusty summer winds.

Perhaps what she most loved about Faro was that he gave her the magic key to leave home. Like a West Texas *Alice in Wonderland*, she was determined to enter the garden of possibilities she had seen through the keyhole vista of her summer visits to Pie Town.

The only objects that she took with her, Doris tells me, were a few clothes and her small hope chest. Inside the chest were two big plates and four small plates she got as prizes from going to the "picture show" in Sweetwater. She tells me that when she and Faro and Pop sat down to eat she would give Pop and Faro the two big plates and take one of the small ones for herself. When Pop was off visiting she got to eat out of the other big plate. Also in the hope chest were a china teapot in the shape of a cat, the cut towels that she had embroidered, and the several quilts that she had made with her mother.

Between Divide and Pie Town

Homesteading was something she understood. She had grown up with her parents' tales of settling West Texas, working the land, raising children, and building a community with churches, schools, and other social activities. Being poor did not frighten her. She had been raised in a loving family, and she was confident of her own ability to love and care for others. For three years she had thought about Pie Town as she attended her classes and did her chores and sat down to dinner with her family. She had imagined being with Faro, building a home, baking bread, going to neighborhood parties, and planting a garden with him. She had seen Faro's family place and knew something of daily life in the Divide community. She was full of pleasure at the prospect of having a place of her own and starting a family.

But the Siberian winter day in 1933 when she arrived in Pie Town with Faro and the Williamses was a difficult time to begin married life. The Depression was at its height, and before long fifteen million Americans were unemployed. During those desperate times, jobless men had deserted over a million women and children. The Plains states, including New Mexico, were especially hard hit. In New Mexico, forty percent of the population was living in poverty, and twenty-eight percent were on relief, the highest percentage of any state in the nation. The percentage was even higher in rural areas. Per capita income was two-thirds of the national average.[11]

The severe and extended drought that caused the Dust Bowl in southwest Kansas and the Oklahoma and Texas panhandles seriously diminished crop production throughout the Southwest. For several years the scorching heat broke all records, and no rain fell on the parched land. Cows died along fences. Crops withered and were not harvested. Banks foreclosed when farmers were unable to pay interest on small notes, and then went bankrupt themselves. In cities and on farms, people were hungry. Work was all but impossible to get, and in the Pie Town area dozens of men were ready to work at the few jobs that became available. Without work or money, daily living was a Sisyphean struggle.

In addition, when Doris arrived at the homestead, she found a very different living situation from the one she had expected. She and Faro had planned to live in Charlie Mickey's house. Faro had made arrangements, but he was broke by the time they arrived home. Neither of them had any money, and they could not find any paying work in the homestead area. The sporadic jobs that surfaced were for men and generally entailed hard labor on roads, at the lumber mills, or on neighboring ranches. Men took their pay, a dollar per day, in whatever anyone had to pay them. They worked for cows, chickens, beans, carrots, cornmeal, feed for their stock, and anything else they could get. Faro had found odd jobs in previous years but he had had to live for long periods of time at neighboring ranches or in town. Now he was reluctant to leave his new bride in the dead of winter.

The climate added to their struggles. Their first winter together the weather was so harsh that even the local sawmills shut down. Doris had always visited in the summer when the sun shone most days and the land greened and blossomed. In winter everything struggled to survive. Because of the altitude on the Continental Divide, Pie Town has a short growing season. Frost can come as early as September and snow can blow across the frozen land until May.

Doris and Faro got to their homestead following a particularly severe winter storm. Doris remembers the warm reception they received when they arrived. They had no place of their own and so stayed a couple of nights with Faro's former stepmother, Lizzie. That first night, a group of their neighbors "shivareed" them. The men stripped Faro down to his underwear and made him trundle Doris in a wheelbarrow in his bare feet through the snow. They also filled their bed with nails. It was uncomfortable and cold, but the community's high spirits made them feel welcome.

Faro immediately went to Pie Town to see if he could borrow money, but shopkeeper Craig would not give it to him. So the only thing Doris and Faro could do was move in with Pop and Loraine, Faro's father and sister.

I wasn't very happy being a bride and moving in with Pop and Loraine. It wasn't real private and I was a new bride. If we had had a room to ourselves I wouldn't have minded. As it was, it was a bad arrangement. They had been batching, and it was the filthiest place you ever saw.

Sam Mickey had given us an axe and a wash pot for a wedding present. Aunt Lizzie gave me some lye soap until I could make my own, so I started. I spent I don't know how many bars of lye soap. You talk about the dirt, the filth. It was terrible. When I arrived as a bride I'd never got in such a mess in my life. I washed several years' accumulation of dirty bedclothes and clothing on a rub board and boiled them in that big black pot. Man, if I had all the clothes I'd boiled in it, I'd be well fixed for clothes to wear.

Little did she know that it would take them almost two years of backbreaking work before they would move on to their own homestead.

In addition, Doris found the Caudills unprepared for the cold months ahead. Under the best of circumstances when crops were adequate, homesteaders worked much of the summer to can and preserve food stores. That summer the drought diminished crop yields. Not only had Pop not washed or cleaned, he had not laid by adequate food for the winter. With no woman in the household all summer, just Pop and the two kids, no one had made the necessary preparations for winter meals. By the time Doris arrived in February, the family's root cellar was nearly empty.

Doris is not a complainer, but she had plenty to complain about. Day in, day out, she and Faro were cooped up in a small room with Pop and Loraine. Pop drank when he could, and twelve-year-old Loraine was too young to be much of a confidant or helper.

Loraine, Faro's younger sister, cannot forget those days any more than Doris can. She suspects that Doris must have thought a lot of Faro to come all the way out to Divide and homestead. Not that Doris arrived with any more money than anyone else did, but she had come from a less arduous life in Sweetwater than the daily struggle they experienced in Divide.

Today Loraine lives in Belen, New Mexico. She and her husband Ben Burns have been married since 1938. For years, Ben played the fiddle for dances all around the Pie Town area. She is a cheerful woman who seems younger than her early seventies. The fall day I stopped to visit with Loraine was mild and bright. She greeted me warmly and then immediately asked me about my last visit with Doris. How was her health? Did she seem in good spirits with all of her husband's difficulties? Although they correspond frequently, the two women have not seen each other for many years, and she was concerned to know more about how Doris was doing. Doris became like an older sister to the motherless Loraine.[12]

Loraine remembers that when Doris arrived at the homestead, the local women thought she was a movie star because she wore make-up and had brought several chiffon party dresses with her from her high school parties in Sweetwater. Doris tells me that she doesn't remember these dresses, but one of Lee's color photographs clearly shows Doris with nail polish. When I ask her about wearing fancy dresses and make-up, Doris vehemently denies it. When I show her the evidence of the photo, she capitulates but assures me that it must have been an atypical moment when the photograph was taken. She says that was not how life was.

Of course Doris was the one who took on the labor of cooking and cleaning on the homestead. She also provided their winter drinking water by melting snow in a pot on the stove, thus saving Faro the labor of hauling it. Nothing fazed her. Ceaseless work gave her something to do in the enclosure of the dark days and spaces.

She was lonely, homesick, and hungry as the snow outside the dugout piled up that winter, heavy as sacks of fresh-milled flour. To walk fifty feet was an effort, and to remain inside and listen to the howling of the wind in the tiny dark room made her feel like a caged coyote.

Since most of her neighbors were Mickey relatives, she knew many of them from her summer visits. It was different, though, being a wife rather than an available young woman. Doris had always made friends easily, but she did not know any of her neighbors as well as she had known Neely Jo and her friends in Sweetwater. She had to form friendships and new relationships, and little by little she did.

From her comfortable Oregon home, she still remembers that winter too well.

> *The first winter of 1933 was definitely the hardest one. It was really difficult. We didn't have practically anything. We went naked and drank branch water and hauled the branch water for a lot of miles.*[13] *We married in February and still hadn't had time to raise a garden or can anything, and I didn't have chickens yet. Our diet was red beans and corn bread for lunch and supper and watery gravy and biscuits for breakfast. After the cows had their spring calves, we finally had milk and butter, but before then it was water gravy.*

When spring finally came, she and Faro rode horseback up on the Largo River above Quemado and stayed a week, helping Uncle Oscar plant corn. Faro plowed and she followed along bare-footed, planting by hand. They were supposed to be working in trade for a cook stove but they never got it, she tells me. She did learn from Huldy how to make a start of sourdough for bread. From then on every winter when milk was scarce they had sourdough bread.

> *That spring and every spring after the first one, I always went out in the fields and pasture and gathered lamb's quarter and canned*

it. It's a green that tastes better than spinach and grows wild. It was one of the first fresh vegetables we had. Later I canned corn and beans, both green and shelled, and anything else we had in the garden. It was too cold and too short a growing season for tomatoes and fruit. Always, just before frost, I gathered everything left and made soup stock. Each year I canned anywhere from five hundred to a thousand quarts of food. That's what we lived on in the winter. As I have said, the first year was the hardest.

Faro owned only three cows to show for the years he had worked before marrying Doris. He traded one of them to the Williamses in exchange for their taking him to Sweetwater to marry Doris. The second one, a white calf, he kept. The third one he took to town that first winter. In order to get the basic supplies they needed, Faro took the cow to Craig at the Pie Town store and mortgaged it for one hundred dollars' worth of groceries. Those cows made the marriage possible and supplied the food they needed for that first winter.

When we lived with Pop, we furnished the groceries. After we finished the year, we went over to town to settle up. We lacked about six or eight dollars, having spent the one hundred dollars. We used it for feed, groceries, sugar. We didn't buy but precious little things out of the store. We never bought anything out of the store that we could raise or that we just did not have to have. We bought sugar, syrup, coffee, tobacco, salt and pepper. We didn't buy any canned goods of any kind, and if we didn't raise vegetables and meat we did without.

None of their immediate neighbors was much better off. Yet, since they had so little, they tried to help one another. No one ever went hungry. "If company came, you just put a little more water in the gravy," Doris tells me.

Everybody pitched in to help each other at harvest time or when someone was ill. One evening, years later, a family's house burned down while they were visiting the Caudills. By that time Doris had an old Model T Ford that had belonged to her grandfather. She says they used to push it more than they drove it, but at least it was better than horseback for getting around.

> *I took Josie and we went all around to the neighbors. I told them that the house had burned down the night before. I came back with that car loaded. This one would give a quilt. That one would give some tea towels they had made. Somebody else would give a pot or a pan. Very few gave food, but a couple did. Then at Pie Town they made up a cash donation for them.*

Faro, too, was generous to a fault. Doris loved that about him. When it came to helping others, he was always ready.

> *Faro had one pair of dress pants that were so thin at the seat you could read a newspaper through them. One time Preacher Hastings, who lived around the mountain a ways, had to go to Albuquerque, and Faro let him borrow his pants because Hastings didn't even have one pair. People kidded Faro about thinking so much of a preacher that he would go into a barrel and loan him his only pair of pants.*

In those early months, it was hard for her even to find the money for stamps to write her mother.

> *I wrote to my mother and she wrote to me. Every once in a while she would send me some stamps in a letter. I wrote once a week, and I'll tell you why. It wasn't too long after I got there that I wrote to the* Magdalena News *and told them that I would write the Divide news if they would send me the stamps. So they sent me stamped envelopes for a period of time. Mine was a separate column headed "Divide" in the paper. Many and many a time, in order to write to my mother I steamed that stamp off that letter that I was supposed to send. Of course I always replaced it by the time I had to send my news in.*

As always, her family helped, saving a little from their meager income to bring to her.

> *My mother would send me things from home, papers. Every time she would send me some papers, we'd build up a great big fire in*

the fireplace and set there. We did not have the money for coal oil
for a lamp so we used the fireplace for light. Sometimes we'd read
all night until we'd read them all. Then, when we got through with
them, I'd take them over and give them to Saunders. They'd read
them and then they would pass them on to the Hamiltons and the
Thomases. Those newspapers would be worn out before they were
finally through reading them. Man, it was something wonderful.

Every once in a while I'd go over to Pie Town and I'd get a
letter. There'd be a dollar bill in it from my mother. You know that
was just like a hundred-dollar bill. It really was, because there
were so many things I could do with that.

Her older sisters Raggie and Callie visited about once a year.
Even though they had little themselves, they would load their cars
down with food, spices, magazines, medicine, and clothes when
they came to visit their little sister. Once they thrilled Josie by
bringing her a tricycle.

Through the first summer, Doris and her family still struggled.
She still remembers with gratitude the visit of her Mama and Dad
in their Buick. They had stopped in Clovis at a fruit store and brought
a hundred-pound sack of potatoes and a watermelon. Mama,
always the provider, had brought them a coop full of hens tied on
the back of the car and some corn she had canned. She also drove
to Pie Town and bought them vinegar, some vanilla and cinnamon,
and some bluing for their clothes. As a special treat, she also bought
Doris a small sack of bulk candy for the family: chocolates, lemon
drops, and Doris's favorite, which she claims she can still taste—
peppermint drops. These were small things, but they went a
long way to sweetening Doris's life, and although she speaks of
her hardships she is quick to sweeten them with the small kindnesses
and simple pleasures that were there, too.

MAKING DO

Doris got pregnant in her second year of marriage. Most of the wives she knew had large families; the Thomases just up the road had twelve children. Housekeeping and childbearing were what women were expected to do, and pregnancy did not mean a woman could work less hard at her daily chores. Prenatal care was nonexistent. Since there were neither doctors nor midwives in the area, childbirth was tended to by other neighborhood women who had little experience other than their own childbearing. A woman who encountered difficulties with her pregnancy or labor either got well or died, depending on her constitution and whatever help her neighbors could offer. With no doctor closer than Socorro, Doris and her mother worried about complications. So the pregnancy was the occasion for Doris's only prolonged absence from Pie Town.

> *Before Josie was born, Mama wanted me to come down to Sweetwater and stay with her, so in May my sister Cal and her husband came out for me, and I went home with them. Money was so scarce, and all the time at Pie Town before she was born I can remember two things about it. I was hungry all the time—I had plenty of red beans and corn bread but I was hungry for something else—and I was constipated all the time. We didn't have a toilet and would always just have to run out in the snow and cold and turn up in the wind. Medicine was an unheard of thing, and with a steady diet of beans and corn bread it was rough. But after I got to Sweetwater, Mama started feeding me fresh vegetables and serving me Milk of Magnesia every night before bedtime.*

Not that her parents did not struggle and make do, also. They had little more than Doris and Faro had. Making do was a fact of life, not a resolution. Doris says she did not realize at the time what they sacrificed for her. She remembers asking her mother for a nickel so that she could buy a big juicy hamburger when she was pregnant. Her mother gave her the nickel and pretended not to wish for one herself. Or, she would offer Doris an ice cream but say she did not feel like one:

> *The things she did without so that I'd have something. Like, she would say, if you would like an ice cream cone—and you could get the biggest ice cream going for a nickel—and she'd say, well, I don't want any. Naturally she wanted some, but she would do without just so that I could have one. I was just a big old kid even then. When Josie was born, I was still a big old knot-headed kid. I can look back now and realize the things she did so that I could have something.*

Doris and Josie

Josie was born on 31 July 1934, at twenty minutes before seven, Doris tells me, in the same room of the same house where she herself was born. The baby had long black hair that needed cutting the minute she was born.

Faro had finished their own half-dugout while she was gone so that they would finally be able to move out from his father's place and have a home of their own. Then he hitchhiked to Sweetwater and arrived just in time for the birth of his daughter. Since he could not leave their animals and crops for long, he had to head back two days later. He managed to get a ride back with Doris's brother Billie:

> *Faro then returned home to Pie town with my brother and his wife. Billie had robbed a grocery store at Menard because his kids were hungry and half-naked. He was caught and sent to the Texas State Penitentiary at Huntsville. I don't remember how long he served, but he got out August 1. August 2, he loaded Toy and the kids and all their earthly possessions in an old Dodge truck and trailer someone had given him, and he started to Pie Town. He had $22 (his veteran's check) and five kids. He came by home and asked Faro if he wanted to go with them. Faro did, and they left about*

sundown with chickens tied on top and Toy and the kids on one
of the mattresses on the back of the truck.

They all laugh today about that trip. It took them eight days
to go from Sweetwater to Pie Town. It was real hot, and those
tires on the truck and trailer were both worn out and rotten.
Faro and Bill changed tires so many times that they used fifteen
cans of tire patching. When they would stop to fix one, there
would always be at least one, sometimes two more, go down
while they were fixing the first one.

Josie was two months old before Doris was able to return to
Pie Town. Nobody had any money to come and get her. Despite
agreeing to her mother's pleas, she had not really wanted to return
to Sweetwater when she got pregnant. She was terribly homesick
for Faro, her new friends, and the homestead. Finally her father
did a small job that earned a few dollars, and her mother drove her
and Josie back.

It was not a good trip. Her mother was sick all the way to Pie
Town. The night they arrived back at the Caudill dugout she passed
out completely with her head drawn back and her eyes popping
out of her head. She was so stiff that Doris and Faro thought she
was dying. Finally they brought her out of the attack, but her health
did not improve. She was so sick the two or three days she stayed
that Doris's brother Billie drove back to Sweetwater with her and
then hitchhiked back to Pie Town.

Medical emergencies were Doris's only fear during those Pie
Town years. She knew that somehow they would make do financially and have enough to eat, but she worried about what would
happen if Faro or Josie had a serious accident or illness. The nearest
doctor was the better part of a day's journey away from where she
lived. Emergencies had to be dealt with by the community without
a doctor's assistance. One day, a neighbor child nearly stepped on a
rattlesnake coiled under the dugout steps. Fortunately, the child
was not bitten, and the rattler was simply killed and hung on the
clothesline, but Doris was alarmed that it might have been Josie
and that she would have been unable to get help, if indeed the

snake had attacked. Danger was not a constant presence, but if an accident or illness did come along, she knew she could only depend on her neighbors for whatever help they could offer.

When anyone got sick, it was one hundred miles to Socorro to a doctor. Most of the time we took care of each other if possible. Mrs. Thomas had twelve children, and only the first one was born with a doctor. All the others except her baby Nita Fay were delivered by Mr. Thomas, and I delivered Nita Fay for them.

Josie at school

Parents did give their children lots of freedom to explore and socialize. Once a child was old enough to ride, he or she would set off with little more than an apple and a tin of kitchen matches in his pocket. He might be gone all day and the parents might not know where he had gone. Young children might walk ten miles through knee-deep snow until their pant legs were frozen just to see each other. If the child got lost or had a problem, like the horse stepping in a hole or breaking a leg, all he did was build a fire and stay put until someone came for him. They all watched out for each other's children.

Nonetheless, Doris worried about Josie. So many children in the rural West died young of minor ailments simply because medical care was too far away. Accidents could happen with little warning.

We dug a well down below the dugout, and it was uncovered like a lot of old wells in that country were and still are. One time when Dad was with us and Josie was about three, we looked out and she was peeping over the side. I called and said, "Josie, come here at once." She started toward the house, and Dad started after her. She turned and ran right toward that well, and Dad never ran so fast in his life and caught her just as she got to the well. Had she fallen into it, it would have killed her instantly. Needless to say, the well was covered that day.

But their biggest scare was a convulsion that, to them, seemed like certain death:

One morning when I was washing dishes and Faro went out to milk, Josie said she wasn't feeling well. She was sitting at the table and hadn't finished her meal. I had my back to her when I heard her fall. She was just two and a half, and I went over to pick her up. She was stiff as a board with her tongue rolled out and her eyes rolled back. She was white as a sheet, and I grabbed her up, screaming "Faro" with every breath, and ran out of the dugout. The snow was deep and about the second step out Faro met me. He had heard me scream and threw his milk bucket over the top of the trees, and we didn't find it for a week.

Josie and friends

We ran all the way to Mrs. Sanders's house in knee-deep snow, first Faro breaking the trail with me carrying her, then me breaking the trail and Faro carrying. I was crying, and Faro was cussing. I don't know. It was about a mile and a half from our dugout to the Sanders's and we got down on our knees in the snow and prayed to God to spare her life. Between crying and praying and running, we took handfuls of snow and rubbed her forehead. She would flinch a little bit, and that was the only way we knew she was still alive. It scared me so bad, kid, even the thought of it still scares me.

Mrs. Sanders heard us coming and met us at her front gate. I said, "Oh, Mrs. Sanders, I think Josie is dying."

She just looked at her and said, "Child, this baby is having a convulsion." We took her into the kitchen where she had some water on in the teakettle. We undressed her and put her whole body in warm water as hot as she could stand and put cold rags on her head.

Faro didn't stop. He kept running out to Claude Holley's to get him to take us to Socorro to the doctor. It didn't seem like he had had enough time to run the two miles over there and get back like he did. By that time, Josie had come out of it, and I had her dressed and waiting. It was the longest miles I ever drove getting her to the doctor in Socorro and just as we got her into the doctor's office, she had another convulsion, but it didn't last as long as the first.

After we left the doctor's office, we got a cup of coffee before starting back, even though we didn't have but just barely enough money to put gas in the car, nothing to eat on. We were the only ones in the café, and a man we had never seen before looked at Josie and said, "My, what a pretty little girl!" He gave her a quarter, a whole great big wonderful quarter. Bessie said to Claude that she wished they had brought their three kids if they had known that.

Before we left Socorro, I wired Dad collect and told him to come, that Josie was real sick. We didn't have any money to eat or anything because we were flat broke. When Dad got my telegram from Socorro—I sent it collect—he got in the car with my two sisters Cal and Raggie. My sister did not have brakes on her car, and here they came from Sweetwater, scared to death. They didn't know but that Josie would be dead when they got there. It's funny now . . . but it was wonderful that they just came. We took Josie to Sweetwater, and she was examined for everything under the sun.

She's never had another one. Those were the main times I really missed a doctor. Other times we just made do.

DIGGING GRAVES

Doris takes another picture out of the basket and then looks away. The image in her hand spawns a dozen more in her memory.

I'd like to go there with you. I know some people in Albuquerque who lived out there. I'd like to take you by and introduce you to them and then make the rounds. Then go on to Pie Town. Probably I don't know a soul there now. I would just love to go out there with you, kid, and rummage around. Wouldn't that be nice? I would know where all the places were. I think I would. Most of them.

Suddenly she is too busy remembering to keep talking. Her voice trails away. She knows that many of her friends from the home-steading years have passed away. I do not know who she is thinking about in particular but I know they are mostly gone, and I start imagining, as though I had been there to witness how it had all happened and their passing.

Finally I break into Doris's musing. Death, too, had to be taken care of by the community. There was no undertaker or funeral home. How had they gone about dealing with someone's death on the homesteads? She responds right away as though we had been discussing it all morning.

One morning as we were eating breakfast, Oscar Schalbar rode up and told us they had just found Grandma Mickey in her bed dead. He was going on to tell some of the neighbors, and Faro was going to tell others. I took Josie to Mrs. Lee's and went on over to Grandma Mickey's house. All that day and night and until 2:00 the next day, I and another lady sat with the corpse and kept rags wet in camphor over her arms and legs and face to preserve her until she could be buried. We dressed her to be buried, and the men went over to the sawmill and got lumber and made her coffin and lined it

with a beautiful black silk dress she had. No one had money or
transportation to take anyone to town if they died, so that's why
they were buried out there at the Divide graveyard behind the school.

Divide cemetery
Photo: Joan Myers

When they were burying their neighbor, Granny Johnson, the community did not dig the hole wide enough at the bottom. The casket got stuck and would not go all the way down into the hole. In order to lower it, they had to remove the casket and dig further down. It was bad luck, she tells me, to have to lift out the casket, and they all knew there would soon be another death. Sure enough, a week later, Granny Johnson's daughter Eula died from eating a can of tuna fish left out open on the kitchen counter. The Divide community came together and buried them side by side in a corner of their old homestead.

Digging graves was a challenge in the hard ground at Pie Town and Divide. Out at the Divide graveyard, the only way to dig a hole big enough for a coffin was to use dynamite. When I chatted with Roy McKee out on his front porch in Pie Town, he leaned back in his chair swing and told me a story about that.

Out there at the Divide Cemetery, that's where Shorty Norton is
buried. Lightning hit him and killed him and his horse, and we had to
bury him there. It was rock hard. He like to spoil before we got him
buried there. We worked on it day and night. We didn't have no
dynamite. General thing later when we had to dig one we'd drill a
hole and shoot 'em. We'd make the hole with dynamite. You'd dig down
part way and it would get so hard you couldn't dig it. Then you'd
shoot it a time or two to loosen it up before you could dig the grave.

When I tell Doris that story, she nods in agreement and then adds:

It was real hard to dig a grave there. The people that was buried
there, there is no danger of anything happening to them. It's a
good hole.

THE LAST FRONTIER

In 1940, the homesteaders of Pie Town, including Doris Caudill, her family, and neighbors in Divide, had visitors who would take them from rural obscurity to public view. Family members or friends visiting from out of town were a common enough occurrence; many families had relatives left in Oklahoma and Texas. But who would have guessed that a government photographer and his wife would come to town and find their life interesting enough to document? Such attention was not something they desired or sought. They certainly could not have guessed that the series of photographs taken of their community would remain as a lasting testimony to their labor, lifestyle, and spirit long after their fields had once again grown over with rabbitbrush and their homesteads had crumbled.

Russell and Jean Lee came through Pie Town in April of 1940, some eleven years after Doris first visited and seven years after Doris and Faro married. They saw the toughness of the place and what it demanded of the homesteaders who farmed there. Intrigued by the name, they stopped along the highway and went into the general store. There they talked to shopkeeper Joe Keele, Craig's partner, and they met the homesteaders who had stopped by that morning for supplies. They overheard discussions about farming, family gossip, and plans for upcoming social events. Excited by the upbeat spirit of the community, Lee saw the possibilities for a photo story. He wrote his boss Roy Stryker back in Washington:

Arrived here yesterday evening after a trip through about all the extremes you could imagine—windstorms, rain, dust storms, sleet, driving snow and finally tropical heat. From Albuquerque we went to Socorro to Datil N. Mex. where we stayed in an old ranch house that had been disassembled piece by piece and rebuilt about ten or

fifteen miles from the original site [the now-destroyed Navajo Lodge].
I took quite a few interiors and exteriors there. Then we crossed
the continental divide and on to Pie Town, which is a settlement
of migrants from Texas and Oklahoma—dry land farmers raising
Pinto Beans and corn. Talked with the store owner there

and I believe it should be one
community we must cover. He
called it the "last frontier" with
people on farms ranging from 30
to 200 acres—some living in cabins
with dirt floors—others better off,
but all seemingly united in an
effort to make their community
really function.[14]

—Russell Lee to Roy Stryker
20 April 1940

Pie Town Hotel

The last frontier, the Wild West, homesteading—these words evoke the
grandest of our national myths: fenceless land, opportunity for
anyone who was willing to work, the satisfaction derived from a
community working together. Lee had been photographing the
effects of the Depression on people in rural Arkansas and the Dust
Bowl in Oklahoma and Texas. It was some of those people who
headed off to California and then got stopped by circumstances in
Pie Town. He wanted to photograph the little town with the
whimsical name where the American Dream was alive and well
despite the hard times.

Back in Washington, D.C., Roy Stryker, Lee's boss and director
of the historical section of the Information Division of the Farm
Security Administration, considered Lee's suggestion. New Deal
programs were mechanizing agriculture and encouraging large-scale
operations, not small farms. Yet the FSA had been created under
the Department of Agriculture to solve the problems of the poorest
farmers, especially those who had lost their livelihood under
New Deal programs. The agency provided grants and loans to aid
tenants in purchasing farms, obtaining health care, and qualifying

for resettlement programs. The FSA was concerned about the westward migration of sharecroppers and tenant farmers and with showing people on the East Coast and the cities how the rural poor were faring. The Pie Town story was hard to resist.

The FSA had no programs for homesteaders, and indeed did not regard homesteading as a viable option for the poor of rural America. But when Stryker thought about Lee's proposal, he realized that Lee's photographs could show a community making the best of hard times and might rally the country behind other agency projects. Stryker

Pie Town road sign

knew that conservatives in Congress were criticizing some of the FSA programs as socialistic and the country as a whole was lukewarm to the plight of underprivileged farmers when so many unemployed people were suffering in the cities.

Stryker had quickly seen the value of photographs in promoting FSA programs. In his early graduate school and teaching days at Columbia, he had worked for Rexford Tugwell, later his boss at the Resettlement Agency, compiling photographs for a book called American *Economic Life*. He soon became familiar with the work of Lewis Hine and other social documentary photographers. He knew that a master like Hine could photograph the harsh conditions of textile mills and glass works in such a way that society could not ignore the problems of the women and children who worked in them. He loved finding photographs that would illustrate abstract ideas. He understood the power of a photograph to connect the viewer to a situation.

Stryker gradually hired and oversaw a small cadre of extraordinarily talented photographers—Walker Evans, Ben Shahn, Carl Mydans, and Dorothea Lange among them. In September 1936, he hired Russell Lee. It was an unlikely choice. Lee had not taken up photography until he was in his thirties and had considerably less experience than anyone else Stryker had hired.

Lee's family was engaged in business, and his early training and work experience were in the field of chemical engineering. However, he had soon found he had little interest in either business or engineering. He left his job as a manufacturing plant manager in 1929 and began dabbling in painting. He studied at the California School of Fine Arts, took some classes with John Sloan in New York, and began spending summers in the artist's colony of Woodstock, New York. Interested in painting portraits but dissatisfied with his drawing skills, he bought a thirty-five-millimeter Contax to record images for his paintings.

Drawing thus brought him to photography, and he soon found himself more interested in photographs than in paintings. His engineering background made him curious about photochemistry and the technical side of cameras and lenses. He soon bought an enlarger, set up a darkroom in his house, and began experimenting with different developer formulas and papers and lighting situations. By the mid-1930s, it was becoming clear to Lee, as it was to many other artists, photographers, and writers, that the hardships of the Depression required more than "art for art's sake." He began shooting people on the streets of New York and coal miners in Pennsylvania, interested in how people lived and worked. Photography, he felt, might help people see and understand the difficulties the country was experiencing.

With a small portfolio of prints in hand, Lee approached Stryker in the summer of 1936. Years later, Lee remembered that meeting. He found Stryker to be friendly and eager to talk about photographs, "but there was no aureole of magic—only the sense that there was a job to be done, that Americans needed to know more about their rural problems, and a general conviction that photographs could play an important role in making rural poverty more visible."[15] Stryker, too, enjoyed the meeting. Despite Lee's lack of experience in the field, Stryker liked the young man and wanted to encourage him. Although he had no opening in the department, Stryker called

Lee within a month to do some freelance photographs of a group of New York tailors the government was trying to settle on a homestead in New Jersey.

Just as Lee delivered these first prints to Washington, Carl Mydans quit the department to work for the about-to-be-published *Life* magazine. Stryker decided to let Lee take his place and soon after sent him on an extended trip to the Midwest to photograph the devastation from the February 1937 flooding of the Ohio and Mississippi Rivers. During the next three months, Lee traveled throughout the upper Midwest. He produced strong images that were widely reproduced by the news services. The quality of the images and Lee's hard work and frequent communications convinced Stryker to hire him full-time. It was the beginning of a powerful body of work that, along with Dorothea Lange's, Arthur Rothstein's and others, has become a touchstone for our collective memories of the Dust Bowl and Depression era.

The two men also began an amiable and long-lasting relationship. Lee advised Stryker on technical matters of cameras, film, and darkroom process. Unlike some of his other colleagues, notably Walker Evans, Lee was a dutiful field photographer. He submitted all the required paperwork and wrote Stryker frequently of his itinerary and intentions. Lee stayed with the FSA until 1942, the longest tenure of any of the eleven photographers who eventually worked for Stryker. He also traveled more miles and took more photographs for the FSA file, over thirty thousand of them, than any of the other photographers. The two men not only respected each other but also became friends. Stryker visited Lee in the field three or four times and took several long trips with Lee and his wife.

Under Stryker's directorship, the FSA eventually produced and maintained a file of over one hundred thousand images and actively promoted the file to news organizations and a variety of external and internal publications. It also produced touring exhibits. By 1940, Stryker could claim an average picture distribution of 1,406 images a month to governmental and private organizations and publications.

As the file grew larger, it acquired a philosophy. Although

Stryker's daily concerns related to the short-term requirements of the FSA in assisting the Department of Agriculture in its policies, he saw that Lee and the other FSA photographers were compiling more than publicity photographs. Stryker began to see himself as a historian-archivist, accumulating images for posterity. He made sure that, unlike photojournalists, the FSA photographers did not have daily emergency deadlines. They were asked to photograph how people responded and felt about their situation rather than just the disaster itself. Or, as Stryker put it, "The magazine and the papers photograph an event; we photograph a condition."[16] The FSA was creating an archive that recorded "the spirit of America at a time of great trial." He believed the collection was an objective look at the country during a time of great change rather than simply a group of images supportive of government policy and programs.

By 1939 Stryker had begun to see the file as a grand record of small-town America and to prompt his photographers to produce more images "on the cheery side." His letters to his photographers in the field, which had always included lists of subjects he wanted covered, now included artistic suggestions on how to shoot them.

In a letter to Russell Lee, dated less than a month before Lee first visited Pie Town, Stryker even suggested that Lee try to take "a few Westons":

> You have no idea how important these highly pictorial syrupy pictures are going to be, especially when someone comes in here who isn't particularly sold on our other photography, and is in a position to go out and do a lot of talking. NM, Ariz., and Utah and the rest of the country do have skies filled with white clouds, so you had better get that red filter out. However, you'd damn well better not go too far, and spoil the picture.
>
> —Roy Stryker to Russell Lee, 28 March 1940

Lee and Stryker joked back and forth about taking photographs in the less documentary, more "artistic" style of Edward Weston, but it was typical of Stryker to spell out his ideas in considerable detail to photographers in the field. To each photographer, he suggested itineraries and discussed possibilities for publication of both completed and prospective images. He expected the photographers to respond with detailed descriptions of what they had just completed photographing and proposals for what they intended to do next. Lee later said:

> *We'd get these letters which would be ten, twelve handwritten pages, something like that. We might get one a week, or every ten days . . . and his observations about the pictures that I had been taking, pictures that Arthur [Rothstein] might have been taking, what Marion Wolcott might have been taking . . . or what Walker Evans was commenting upon . . . It was very valuable to note these.*[17]

Although Lee's photographs have become icons of their particular time and place, he was not working for himself. He was not getting support from a patron, like some Renaissance painter, to make art out of his creative impulses. Lee was salaried to produce photographs for Stryker's very specific purposes and was a willing associate.

Jean Lee, his wife and companion on most of his FSA assignments, explained it this way:

> *These photographs were designed to show people what was happening in other parts of the country. It was also to influence the Congress to appropriate more money in areas where people really needed it. They worked. They were used by newspapers and magazines and all sorts of places. The Congressmen saw them and it kept money coming for FSA projects.*[18]

Stryker knew that Lee could photograph Pie Town in such a way that those who saw the photographs would empathize with the struggles of rural America. On 22 April 1940, by return mail, he answered Lee's initial Pie Town proposal in a characteristically pragmatic and questioning fashion:

> *Pie Town sounds most interesting. By all means put it on your agenda. If, after you have sampled it, it still seems as good a story as you indicate, then we should encourage someone to write it up, and offer them the pictures to go with it. I am always rather skittish*

about Collier's *but perhaps we could get them to do it. If not,* Look, *or perhaps* The New York Times Magazine. *You will, of course, get a pretty complete story on it, which we could submit to any of these agencies. The photographs, as far as possible, will have to indicate something of what you suggest in your letter, namely: an attempt to integrate their lives on this type of land in such a way as to stay off the highways and the relief rolls. I suppose the store-keeper was right—a "last frontier." I suspect you had better look pretty carefully under this phrase. Sometimes we get fooled by these "last frontiers."*

We are going to need quite a few pictures of the people: close-ups of faces, interiors of their homes, something of their farming life.

—Roy Stryker to Russell Lee, 22 April 1940

Encouraged by Stryker's response to his proposal, Lee arranged his itinerary so that a few weeks later he and his wife Jean were in Pie Town. His letter to Stryker expresses his enthusiasm:

Next Sunday at Pietown they are having a big community sing— with food and drink as well; it lasts all day so I'm going to be sure to be here for that. Have also discovered that they are cutting in these here mountains by means of the broad axe, so I'll get that when I return. Also there will probably be a big square dance a week from Tuesday here.

Everything's going fine. There will be more pictures of Pie Town to follow. Most of the work I've done so far has been in the country. There are a few more shots needed in the town here, which I'll get next weekend. Haven't had a bath—outside of sponge bath—for ten days, so I'm sure going to welcome a shower.

—Russell Lee to Roy Stryker, 9 May 1940

THE PHOTOGRAPHER AND HIS WIFE

When Lee and his wife Jean returned to Pie Town in early May of 1940 to begin photographing, they brought a car full of photographic equipment with them. For shooting, Lee used a 9-by-12-centimeter Linhof Technika with a 3¼-by 4¼-inch back, a 3¼-by-4¼-inch Anniversary Speed Graphic, and two Contax 35-millimeter cameras—one with a normal focal length lens and the other with a slightly wider lens. He also had hundreds of sheets of cut film, cut film holders, cases of 35-millimeter roll film, tripods, and equipment for field developing black-and-white film. (Lee occasionally processed a small portion of his film in his hotel bathrooms, so he could immediately check the results. The rest of the processing and all the printing were done in Washington at the government lab.) Flash bulbs were newly available, and Lee carried three flash guns and cases of flashbulbs, as big as light bulbs but much safer than the old-fashioned magnesium powder that had to be lit on a plate. Their '38 Chevy bulged with all the gear they had to carry.

For Russell and Jean, Pie Town was unlike the daily grind of assignment shots they had been doing for Stryker, with only a night or two spent in any one location. They had just completed a series of photographs in the Phoenix area. "A most modern community," Lee wrote to Stryker, with beautiful schools, lawns, stores, swimming pools, and irrigated crops. Modern, but not very exciting photographically. The Lees immediately perceived that Pie Town provided considerably more visual interest than the farms and swimming pools of Phoenix.

They visited Pie Town off and on over a six-week period and also traveled to Mogollon, New Mexico, to shoot the miners, and to neighboring Quemado for the rodeo. During that time, the Lees observed and photographed homesteaders plowing fields, planting crops, having picnics, and playing the domino game "forty-two."

They attended community sings, Farm Bureau meetings, and school sessions. They both enjoyed their stay, and so Russell shot a lot of pictures, Jean says. Their visits provided a working vacation.

As a result, more than six hundred images of Pie Town exist today in the Library of Congress. Most of them are black-and-white, but seventy-two are in color. Kodachrome color slide film had been introduced two years previously and was made available in small quantities to the FSA photographers. For the most part the color images duplicate work that Lee shot more extensively in black-and-white.

Lee describes his approach to his subject matter in the *U.S. Camera* article published a little over a year after his visit. When he started work on Pie Town, he began by getting long shots and close-ups of the different businesses. He was fascinated by the general store:

> *Not only did it harbor all sorts of groceries, fruits, meats, but medicines, clothing, seeds were carried in stock. Farmers sat around inside talking. The heavy store scales were used by all to see if they were gaining or losing. . . . There was plenty of activity among the shopkeeper and his staff—selling goods, packaging, cleaning up, buying from the itinerant trucker, working over the accounts, and even selling fishing licenses. One of the girls in the store was an expert hairdresser who did a good business.*[19]

He wrote Stryker:

> *Am getting my lineup on work around here this afternoon and expect to have about 5 full days' work here—there is a big meeting of surrounding farmers here Saturday night (Farm Bureau) and on Sunday there should be church services. I think there's going to be a good story here but it certainly looks like the last frontier here—even the hotel rooms are furnished with only a bed, a table, a chair and a "thundermug." No baths are available.*
>
> —Russell Lee to Roy Stryker, 30 May 1940

Out in the countryside, Lee began photographing the homesteaders of Divide, Doris's immediate community, located twelve miles south of Pie Town. Although Doris and her neighbors rarely socialized with those in town because the distance was too great for them to travel easily, Jean says that they called the whole area Pie Town because "there wasn't any other town."

Lee outlined the work to be done: the terrain, the homesteads, the farm tools, clothes, food and schools, the social life of the community. How did people get along without much money? How did they feel about this part of the country—did they want to stay or to go back to Texas or Oklahoma or to move on? He needed long shots of the terrain and he remembered Stryker's request that he get close-ups of people, the inside of their homes and "something of their farming life."

Doris tells me that she saw Lee and Jean often when they were in her area, and her assertion is backed up by the more than one hundred images in the file that Lee took of her and her family. I suspect that she provided a headquarters for his work "in the country."

> *Lee didn't stay with us. He had this place over at Pie Town at the hotel. He came to our house, and he would come early and stay all day. I was the one who told him about the dances we had and all the things, and he thought they were fascinating. He wanted to get in on it, which was fine. I'm sure that poor old Lee thought we were characters.*

Often, she says, they came for lunch or dinner and she would tell them who was having a party, or that the children were having a special program at the school, or that Mrs. Staggs had just made a beautiful quilt. She liked the Lees, especially Jean, who was a fellow Texan.

> *I loved both of them. They were just real nice people. They were so down-to-earth, our kind of people. They weren't snobbish or high-toned. Some people that came out there, like peddlers, for instance, they would act like if they touched anything, they'd get c-r-a-p. We were human beings even though we didn't have anything. The Lees were just real good people.*

She recalls that the process of being photographed by Lee was a comfortable one. He stayed in the background, close by but invisible. "You didn't even hardly realize that he was doing it." She did note that Russell was always thinking about his next picture and wanting to get up and work rather than sit around and talk.

They would stay at a meal at our house, but he would make Jean get up and move. He'd say, "The government is paying me to make pictures, but not of my wife. I could do that anywhere anytime."

Russell had grown up in small-town Illinois and knew rural people well. In Pie Town, as in other projects and years later when he was a teacher, he had a gift for putting others at ease. He cared for people, smiled easily, and had a natural candor that immediately made people feel comfortable being themselves. He phrased it himself, modestly, "If I saw a good picture, I'd take it. They didn't even know I was there for a while, really, people just get intent."[20]

Jean Lee was an unsung collaborator in the ongoing process of exposing the details of a homesteading life. Born Jean Smith in Vernon, Texas, in 1908, she grew up in Dallas where her father was district manager for Southwestern Bell. She began writing for the *Dallas Times-Herald* while in high school and wrote a regular column on campus activities while attending Southern Methodist University in Dallas. Much later she was to put her organizational talents to work as campaign manager for Senator Ralph Yarborough in his 1952 and 1954 campaigns for Governor. Texas Governor Ann Richards later referred to her as "my role model, a woman of extraordinary talent and a good fighter."[21]

"She could get anyone talking," Russell said. Her warm conversation and easy way with strangers freed Russell to work and she accompanied her husband throughout his FSA travels. Her journalism background made her a natural editor for the photographs. She also took on the responsibility for all the text and captions for the Pie Town photographs. This was not a minor task since Stryker insisted that each picture in the FSA file have a detailed caption: "The photograph is only the subsidiary, the little brother of the word. . . . In truth there's only one picture in a hundred thousand that can stand alone as a piece of communication," he was fond of saying.[22] Jean Lee's role was thus that of working partner with her husband, a role that Russell always warmly acknowledged but that has been little recognized by FSA historians or art critics.

Stryker's directive had been to show that the homesteaders were succeeding in their "attempt to integrate their lives on this type of land in such a way as to stay off the highways and the relief rolls," and Lee's enthusiasm for the task is evident in his letters. How did Lee approach the assignment? Certainly Stryker's instructions were seductive. How well were the homesteaders really succeeding? How did Lee feel privately? Jean Lee has answers to these questions.

Over the phone, Jean Lee expresses bemusement and surprise that I want to come to Austin to interview her. When I arrive at her apartment, she welcomes me warmly. Her legs and heart are failing, she tells me, but for all that she seems an extraordinarily youthful eighty-eight years old. Like Doris, Jean is an easy storyteller with an old-fashioned Texas twang, and her memories of the FSA years come easily.

Russell died in 1986 at the age of eighty-three after many years of teaching photography at the University of Texas at Austin, she tells me, and she has continued living there after his death.

She had studied journalism in college and was a stringer for *Time* magazine in New Orleans when a writer friend introduced her to Russell. He was five years older than she and had been married before, but the couple had grown apart with all Russell's travel. He had begun working for the FSA and shared some of his enthusiasm and experiences with Jean. "It didn't take fifteen seconds," she tells me, "for us to know we belonged together." "Without the vaguest idea of what I was getting into," she took off with him.

Like Doris, she could have married a local boy and stayed home in a comfortable, ordinary life. But she did not. She just closed her

Jean Lee
Photo: Joan Myers

apartment and set off. Both Doris and Jean tended toward caution in the small decisions of their life, but in the big ones, they followed their hearts and leaped.

When Jean and Lee set off, it was 1937, the depths of the Depression. In 1938, they went to Mexico to get married and then continued to travel until Russell joined the Air Force in 1943. They had no home of their own, but they loved being on the road together. The longest they ever stayed any one place was when they went back to FSA headquarters in Washington, D.C., but that was only for a month or so maybe once a year. Then they were back on the road.

When we arrived in Pie Town, there wasn't much on that little main street. There was a little place that sold souvenir things . . . and a community building on the same side of the street. I don't think there was any place to go to school; I think they used the community building. There was also a church on the right-hand side of the highway. On the right-hand side was a filling station, not much, and the little hotel. On the other side of the street was Mr. Craig and Mr. Keele's general store and this café run by Lois and Harvey. We ate there. If they were busy doing something else, we went in the kitchen and got ourselves some coffee.

We stayed at the hotel. It had two rooms in it, very small little rooms. In the tiny lobby was a stove. One day I baked a cake in that old wood stove. When we wanted to take a bath, we'd heat water in a tub on it.

The privy was across Highway 60. To go to the bathroom you had to cross Highway 60 to the privy. The hotel didn't have its own privy—that was the town privy.[23]

Russell and Jean rented the only two rooms in the hotel, and Russell improvised a darkroom in one of them by sealing the windows with newspaper and blankets. Here, he would take an hour at the end of a busy day of shooting to change film. Lee's letters to and from Stryker, as well as his exposed film, traveled by the "stage," a car fitted up with roof rack and expanded fenders for carrying everything from the mail and sundry supplies to suitcases and crates of live chickens. It made the 130-mile round trip between Pie Town and the railroad at Magdalena every day. Pie Town had no telegraph or telephone at the time of the Lee's visit (telephone service did not arrive in town until late 1963).

Russell and Jean enjoyed the freedom of setting their own work times, though in practice that often meant they worked every day they were not traveling. They were often even busier on the weekend than during the week, because that was when more families were at home together or involved in community activities. Jean tells me that they did not mind the inconveniences. They were young. Not having a shower does not matter much when you are only in your thirties.

Pie Town Hotel
Photo: Joan Myers

One afternoon, they relaxed and made ice cream with Harvey and Lois Stagg who ran the café:

> *There was a man who lived some fifteen or twenty miles away who cut ice from the river in the wintertime and stored it in a house made of wooden blocks. He wrapped it up in straw and sawdust and stuff. We were working in that area and bought a hunk of ice from him. Lois and her mother mixed up some stuff to make ice cream. There are some photographs in the file of Harvey squatting down on his haunches grinding ice cream. Everybody who lived there near the café ate some.*

They were interested in how people were living, Jean tells me. Pie Town was special because it was one of the last homesteading locations in the country.

> *It was all homesteading out there. One guy homesteaded a hundred feet from the main store. You could spit to where he was. He had children, and everyone in town helped him build a little house. They had arrived with no money. His house was of those split logs. The*

only thing he had to buy was fifteen cents worth of nails. There were lots of folks who walked barefoot and put their shoes on just when they were coming to church.

Pie Town was fascinating to the Lees and to Stryker because people were enacting the role of pioneers in the legendary drama of a frontier community. Although the Depression was a desperate time, the days when a family could clear a patch of land, raise a few crops, and be contentedly self-sufficient were over in the rest of the country. The country was settled. It was a finished nation, not an emerging one. But in Pie Town, settlers lived more in the nineteenth century than in the twentieth, without telephones, electricity, or running water.

It was a hard life, but I don't think they considered it a particularly hard life at the time. There was a lot of self-entertainment there— the forty-two parties [a domino game], holiday singing, church on Sundays, bringing picnic lunches. It was a sociable sort of area for people. There were all sorts of musicians. They worked hard but they also played hard, and they didn't have much to play with. They had to do it themselves.

After completing his Pie Town photographs, Lee moved on to other FSA projects: He worked in a government unit that recorded aerial navigation routes during World War II, he documented conditions in America's coal mines for the Department of the Interior, and he joined Roy Stryker in a large documentary project on Standard Oil. Russ did not have any interest in exhibitions, Jean says, or any concern for photography as an art form. He did not see his photographs as art, and he did not see his Pie Town images as any better or worse than any other photographs he did in his life. His images of Pie Town appeared in a handful of magazine articles but were not exhibited as art until a 1982 show at the Lee Witkin Gallery in New York.

The sudden attention from the art world puzzled Russell, as did seeing his photographs enshrined as art objects.

The fact that these photographs became what people call "works of art" was something that happened, but it was not at all the purpose, nor was it of any interest to any of the photographers.

As far as I know Russ had no pride one way or another in these photographs. It was just a job. He just enjoyed doing it. He showed no indication of being interested one way or another after he saw the negatives. If he were asked something about a particular negative, he'd say, "Well, I got an image."

Art aside, Lee was aware of the importance of his role in documenting a particular place and time. His photographs were made for use, to convey information. He knew his photographs could convey the spirit of the area to the rest of the country. "I got excited about it," he said in a 1985 interview, "because it seemed to me this was the sort of place that had unalterably molded the American character."[24]

A TYPICAL DAY

When I look at Lee's portrait of the Caudill family seated on their living-room couch, I see how close they were. Doris is the center of the group with Josie on one side with her elbow in Doris's lap and Faro on the other, almost sliding into her. Behind them is the foot-wide shelf of the half-dugout and its plastered walls. Doris had taken pages from large magazines like the *Saturday Evening Post* and stuck them up on the walls with a flour-and-water paste. She has a faint smile on her face and looks to one side of the camera, while Faro looks down at her arms. In one hand, he holds his large broad-brimmed hat and in the other the armrest of the couch, as if he is falling away from it, toward her. Faro's shirt is dirty, and his pants are rolled up; his hat is stained. Doris still has her flour-sack apron on over her skirt and blouse. They both look like they have just finished a hard morning's work. I sense how strong Doris was in the family from how Faro and Josie lean into her on the decrepit couch.

A typical day? Faro got up and would milk the cows while I cooked breakfast. We just kept getting more cows until we had six or seven.

After breakfast, we would both go out . . . if it was time to get the crop in, we'd do that . . . pinto beans and corn. The corn we grew in that country was not big corn because it wouldn't mature in that short a season. It was this little Mexican Indian squaw corn. Sometimes you'd almost have to dig it out because it grew so close to the ground. It was good and had a lot of strength in it for the animals. The pinto beans was a cash crop when we made any. That was why we kept wanting to clear more land so that we could have a bigger area to get a source of income.

I washed on a washboard. I boiled my clothes in an iron pot. On the days I washed I had to take the beds out to sun, and I'd

take the mattress out to the yard. At noon I'd go out and take the
broom, and man, I'd beat it and then turn it over. At night I'd bring
it back in and it was real nice.

The Caudills in front
of the dugout

On an ordinary day, both Doris and Faro shared the outdoor work, and Doris had the indoor work as well. When Faro could find it, he worked at day labor while Doris did all the household chores.

Russell Lee photographed the Caudills' daily routine. Several images show Doris straining milk from a tin bucket through a large funnel into a glass jar. In another image, she places the jar into a homemade cooling box made of rough pine and screening. Damp cloths are wrapped around the jars of milk, keeping them cool through rapid evaporation in the open air. The box is in the shade under a large pine. Doris, her back to the camera, is lifting a hinged wood flap to put the milk in. She wears a short-sleeved checked blouse, a dark skirt, and an apron. She wears heavy hose and laced-up leather shoes with a slight heel. The outfit seems too delicate for farm work. The photograph is so detailed that I feel I am standing there, drinking fresh milk in the hot sun.

Lee's photograph does not begin to show how hard Doris worked. Cooling the milk was only the beginning of the process. Next, she would skim off the cream. Another of Lee's images shows a post with tin coffee cans and pails hanging from it; among the cans are the parts to the cream separator that Doris used to skim cream. After the separating, she would churn the cream into butter.

Each day she would make cottage cheese from the milk of the day before. While she was cooking breakfast, she would put a gallon of the day-old clabbered milk on the back of the warm stove where the clabber would separate further from the whey. Then she would put the curds in a towel and hang them on the clothesline until they dripped dry. She made cottage cheese fresh every day and tells me they would have starved if she had not.

Unfortunately, she tells me, "Those cows were so poor you had to prop them up to milk them, and needless to say they didn't give much milk. Poor old things. We had to prop them up to milk them," she says.

Doris cooked, did laundry, ironed, and cleaned up. When I ask her how she kept a dirt-floored dugout clean, she tells me that she would pour the last of the dishwater rinse on the floor and sweep it. "Not too sanitary," she laughs. Meanwhile Faro did the water hauling and heaviest garden work. They both grubbed rabbitbrush, trying to clear more land for gardening and a bean and corn crop.

We pulled the rabbitbrush out by hand with a grubbing hoe. You just bent down and kept grubbing at those roots, and kept grubbing and finally you got the roots. Faro would chop the trees down, and then we would build a great big fire around the trunk. It took more than once. You didn't clear trees the first year. It was two or three years sometimes before you got the stumps out enough that you could plow. Yes, it was hard work. Nothing was easy on the homestead, hon.

After a break for lunch, they would clear more land and work in the garden. Josie followed along as soon as she could walk. The family needed all the land they could clear for their own vegetables and to grow a pinto bean crop they could sell for a little cash. If they got enough moisture from snow and rain, they could grow about five hundred pounds of beans on each acre. They would pick and thresh them by hand and then sell them for four to six cents per pound to Harmon Craig in Pie Town. By the time Lee photographed their homestead, the Caudills had about fifty acres of their section cleared with about thirty acres in pintos and the rest in feed crops and vegetables.

Doris's mother sent her a pressure cooker, which was a considerable help in preserving the vegetables they grew each summer. Pressure processing of vegetables took time, but much less time than processing in a boiling water bath, and it offered considerably greater safety. Only a third of rural New Mexico women had electricity by 1940, unlike their urban counterparts who already had washing machines, refrigerators, and electric irons. They could not afford to buy their food in cans, like most urban women, and the pressure cooker was the first major improvement in their kitchen equipment. Jean Lee recounts that the FSA budgeted money to help rural women buy jars and cookers. "The pressure cooker is so important there ought to be a picture of it on our national flag," one woman told her.

One of Lee's photographs shows Doris in the process of packing up her kitchen apparatus in preparation for dismantling and moving the dugout. The pressure cooker is clearly visible next to two small wooden boxes of cans, jars, and a couple of cast-iron skillets that are her only other kitchen equipment. Many a time, Doris sat up late at night with only the red glow of the wood stove for company, "waiting for the cooker to go to full time," and then bit by bit to release pressure.

Late in the afternoon, it would be time to stop outside work and bring in the cows. This was usually Doris's job since Faro was stronger than she was and could continue doing more of the heavy work. She would listen for the cowbell and then lead the cows home for milking. She still has the cowbell hanging on a hook in her kitchen in Cascade Locks and she rang it for me. After milking, they would have supper. Since oil for the lamps was expensive, they would usually go to bed when it got dark.

The men shot game when they could find it.

Out on the plains going from Alegra Mountain to Quemado was a great big windmill. That windmill was an old rundown homestead that belonged to the Bates. They had three or four boys. When my brother came out the first time, we went to Quemado. On the way back, just before we got to the Bates place, we saw these antelope. My brother had a gun and Faro had borrowed a gun. I was driving his car, which was a Model A Ford, and my brother was on one side and Faro on the other. I'd drive just as fast as I could to get up close to the antelope and they'd holler stop. I'd stop right straight and then they'd jump off and try and shoot the antelope, but their guns wouldn't reach that far. One time my brother hollered stop, and when I set the brake Faro went tumbling head over heels right out in the boonie goonies.

One time we were pretty close to the Bates place and I looked up and there was somebody on a horse, one of the Bates boys who was mowing hay. He was out there mowing and when we came doing all that shooting it was just like an army shooting. I looked up and he was on his horse, just beating that horse as hard as he could, running to get away. Man, we had a lot of interesting things.

Food was hard to come by, and shooting deer out of season was common practice. Faro did not own a gun, so he did not hunt. Others, like neighbors Work and Whittie Reed, hunted for antelope out on the plains west of Alegra Mountain. It was a special occasion when they came to visit, with fresh meat tied on their saddles. Doris never asked them what it was or where they got it. The family just ate it and enjoyed it even though, Doris tells me, the antelope meat was "too old and tough to stick a fork in."

If Faro was lucky enough to find work, he would be gone during the day. Occasionally he found cowboy work at the Dahl Ranch a few miles away, trimming brush, moving cattle from range to range, or branding. Faro would take a day's work here and there, anything that he could find. Often the work was not paid in cash but in seed corn or carrots. During the time the Lees were in town, Faro had a part-time job working for Herman Craig, who was building a warehouse to store the local pinto bean crop. Another time, he went off for a month during the winter and cut fence posts for cash. In the fall, everyone gathered piñon nuts—the Zuni and Navajos came every year to harvest them, and the homesteaders could often make a little cash gathering them as well. The trees only bore nuts every four or five years, so they could not be depended on for a regular income, but when they did, homesteaders could make six to eight cents a pound. Although homesteaders could build dugouts and grow some food with their own labor, a cash income was essential—for the cast-iron stove and other kitchen supplies, for some clothes, for food staples such as flour and sugar, and for any extras like the radio the Caudills managed to buy.

While Faro was gone, Doris had to fill in and do his tasks as well as her own.

Women had to work, right up beside the man, just as hard as men all day. Then when you came home at night, your woman's work was still there, the cooking and everything else. The man could smoke his RJR and put his chair back and relax a little. If there was any luxury like a sack of RJR tobacco, well, who got the luxury? It was the man instead of the woman. Also, the man would get out more, go to town more often.

For the Caudill family, the years passed according to the rhythms of the land. Josie grew up, while Faro and Doris got a little ahead one year, then fell behind the next. It was a life of daily hard work and few possessions.

I saved all my sugar sacks and flour sacks and made clothes out of them. They were real pretty, and I made Josie's pants out of the sugar sacks and used old pieces of inner tube for the elastic. I did not know how to sew and didn't have a machine, but what I did, I did with my fingers.

Everybody that could sew did, but I would do a lot of patching. I patched patches on top of patches. I made quilts but not dresses. One time my sister Raggie sent me fourteen little dresses for Josie that she had made out of scraps sewing for other people. There were two of yellow organdy and one of green silk that I remember in particular. She's wearing one of them in the Lees' photographs.

Josie was five years old when Lee came to photograph. In one image, she sits on the ground next to a tree trunk and gathers pine pitch to use as gum. In another, she looks pensively over a picket fence, one hand grasping a rough-cut pine board and the other elbow coming over the top. This time, her hair is uncombed and her forehead furrowed as she looks off into the distance. Doris says he followed her around to photograph her playing with her toys, combing her hair, and going to school.

In another photograph, Josie is looking in a large three-piece mirror and brushing her hair. The mirror is part of a dressing table with turned legs that Doris used as a child. Her sister Raggie brought it out for Doris all the way from Sweetwater. Doris says it was the only special piece of furniture they had. Josie stands before the mirror in dirty shoes and socks, a sweater with a rip under the arm, and a ragged checked skirt. Behind the dressing table is the foot-wide shelf that went the whole length of the dugout. The wall is covered with layers of oilcloth and cardboard to keep out the cold air. On one side is a Chinese checkers board that they would all play in their spare time in the evenings. On the other side is a large bottle of Watkins Red Liniment, which they used on cow teats when they were sore or on themselves when they got an inflammation or scrape.

Mirrors this size were a novelty for the homesteaders in the area. Everybody who came by stepped up to look at themselves, much as we do today with the security camera in the Seven-Eleven store.

When the Reed boys, Whittie, Work, and Bill, came by, they always sat next to the mirror, and every chance they got when they thought no one was looking, they would look at themselves in that mirror. I'll always have a real soft spot in my heart for them.

Doris keeps saying she knew they would manage even in the hardest times. She remembers one day when she and Neely Jo, who was visiting her friend, were outside doing the wash. She would wring out the clothes and hand them to Neely Jo to hang over the fence to dry. She remembers starting to laugh and saying to Neely Jo, "I've heard of an empty gut and a bare butt, but this beats all I've ever seen." She held up a pair of Faro's long underwear, and it did not have any seat left in it.

Another time Faro got down to where he only had this one pair of pants and one shirt that was so patched you could hardly tell what they were. Just having one shirt I couldn't keep him clean, so I wrote to my sister-in-law Ruth and asked her if she would send him another shirt. I asked for an old one of my brother Buster's, but by return mail she sent us two—brand new. We felt like millionaires.

She had confidence in her ability to pilot her own life as well as a belief that a greater power was in charge. I ask her where she got that kind of faith and if she didn't think the land was especially hard on women. Doris laughs, not because it is funny, but because it is hard to explain. When you worry, she says, you get old and wrinkled. You don't want that, do you?

Do you know what gout is? I never heard of it before. I always remembered these pictures of Maggie and Jiggs and Jiggs was big and fat and he had a cigar in one hand and his foot all propped up and a drink in the other. Well, I don't drink or smoke, but I tell you, from the bottom of my toe up to my knee was just as black and so swollen. My leg was so swollen that it didn't anymore look like a leg. You couldn't even tell I had toes because it was such so swollen. It's gone down now, but it still hurts. I try and ignore it as much as I can. I have been on crutches. I'm just now beginning to walk. Every time I open my eyes and I'm alive I'm real grateful. It's a brand new world.

Also, my husband's not too good, hon. He hasn't been well . . . and my Josie, her husband is dying with melanoma cancer. It's just one thing right after another.

I've just been lying in bed looking at the ceiling and feeling sorry for myself because I can't do anything. I've felt so low I could crawl under a snake's belly with a high felt hat and never touch a hair. The Sunday before last was the very living end. I just broke down and cried and cried and cried and felt sorry for myself all day. Ever since then I've been so much better, mentally and physically and every other way.

DANCING UP A STORM

Arrived here yesterday a.m. and got a good set on the community singing. Tonight am going to a square dance—tomorrow broad axe work. —Lee to Stryker, 17 June 1940

Looking at Lee's photos, I am especially curious about the images of the community events. These were days without television or movie theaters. Recreation, like everything else, was something you had to do yourself.

Doris and Faro

Although Doris and her family and neighbors labored all day, they looked forward to evenings and weekends as an opportunity to have a good time together. From her stories and Lee's photos, it is possible to reconstruct some of these events.

Doris and her family were able to afford a radio after several years of hard work. One Christmas, when Josie was two years old, the family went to Albuquerque. It was the only time they had enough money to go shopping out of Pie Town during the thirteen years they lived in Divide. They went to Montgomery Ward's and bought a battery-powered radio, the only one in the community for many years. They put the radio on the shelf that separated the ground-level dugout from the logs stacked above; it was a favorite place for putting things. It was the first radio that some in the community had ever heard, and it became the focus of community activity, a sort of stand-in storyteller.

When the war broke out in Europe, Pop would back his chair up so his head was right next to it and listen as closely as he could. "I'll listen to the news," he would say.

One night, Granny and Jo were there and we were listening to a gospel service coming from Oklahoma City. After it was over, she said to me, "Doris, every day more of the Bible is revealed to us. I have often read the passage that says his word will be shouted from the rooftops, and I never knew what that meant until now. Just think how long ago that was written and now since radios are invented and the sound comes from our rooftop, it's just as plain as day."

Every Friday night people met at a different house to play forty-two, a domino game favored especially by Texans and Okies. Doris and many of her neighbors had learned the game in their childhood, and they loved to play it for hours. Roy's daughter Kathryn describes it to me as akin to bridge in that it was played with partners. Each person was dealt seven dominoes and then they bid on the doubles. Often they played dominoes and the card game pitch until the radio stations went off the air.

Our neighbors didn't realize it because they would only come one night a week maybe, but someone was there each night. They would rotate on us, but we were up every night. I laugh and say, well, we lost one crop because we were playing pitch. We lost another six because we were playing forty-two. We had fun every night and then slept late the next morning. It's kind of silly now.

Doris was a prime mover for Divide's Literary Society, which met every two weeks. She rounded up adults and children alike to act in plays, recite verses, sing songs, and stage debates.

One night, she and Ozella Fowler debated Harvey Hamilton and Claude Holley about whether a cow or a chicken was more important. The men argued for the chicken and the women for the cow, everybody listing the good points for his or her favorite animal. Doris made a case for all the things cows were used for and their by-products. She listed all the uses for cow chips, from fertilizer to shade for plants, and when she said, "and if you smoke," she brought down the house.

She and Ozella won the debate.

Lee photographed a meeting of the Literary Society held at the Divide schoolhouse. In one image Doris and Faro are both singing along with several of their neighbors. Another is a close-up of Doris singing while an older man with glasses holds the kerosene lamp for her. A caption says: "Mr. Beeson, president of the Literary society, holds the lamp for Mrs. Caudill, secretary, during a song at the Literary society." In the absence of electric light, Lee had tried out his new flash bulbs. (The resulting effect pleased neither Lee nor Stryker who complained after seeing the images that "Your flash shots gave a completely unnatural illumination which as you remember made the picture appear a little bit ridiculous—here was a man obviously struggling to read by this poor light—and yet the room was almost as brilliant as day-light.")[25]

4-H encampment

Birthdays were special occasions and were celebrated with an all-day Sunday visit after the birthday. Lee photographed one of these lazy afternoons at the Caudills' neighbors. Everyone is sitting around the front yard, talking. Doris is sitting in the doorway, her hat below her on the ground, with Molly and Oleta Fowler looking at her. Josie is on a small tricycle, and other kids are sitting by their parents or playing in the dust, laying out farms with miniature terraces just as their parents did in real life. Faro is squatting in the shade, rolling a cigarette and, no doubt, telling tall tales to his neighbors.

Other events were seasonal. At the Divide school Christmas program, Doris and Faro would make the whole community laugh by wrapping up presents for all the men:

> . . . *the neck of a hen, a dirty dishrag, old worn-out pants, an empty vitamin bottle—anything to get a laugh. . . . Just before Christmas we would have a pie supper. We didn't have much money, but that would bring in enough that we would get bags for everybody with some nuts and an apple and an orange and a little bit of candy.*

Sometimes it wasn't much but it was that much. A lot of times that was all the Christmas some kids in the community got.

The idea of having fun today is not such a community affair, nor is it do-it-yourself. I ask Doris how she sees the difference.

My great granddaughters . . . I've got two of them . . . they've got to have those great big long claws put on their hands that look so awful. They just look terrible to me. But that's the thing they want. Well, that takes money or they don't do it. It's the same thing anywhere they go or whatever they do. It's something that requires a lot of money. We really had a good time without money. I still would if I could. I'd get me a group that would play forty-two and we'd come to each other's house and things like that.

I don't remember ever being by ourselves in the nine and a half years we lived there. We never had much in material possessions, but we had lots and lots of friends and never did we ever sit down to a meal by ourselves. There were few nights that there were not wall-to-wall pallets. I even made a bed under the table.

Times have changed. Today, despite socializing with her local church group, her neighbors, and her VFW volunteer friends, Doris knows the days of community entertainment are gone. People think they are too busy to spend time together except for a limited number of carefully planned events. Even most of her grandkids are too busy to spend time with their grandmother. Today, a concert or a play requires professional musicians or actors. Back then, community was something in which you expected to participate.

Doris looks at the Lee photos and tells me:

This was at a dance we had at the Staggs's. I wish we were out there and I could show you where. After you left the Dahl's house, you went toward the mountain on a long lane that went from their house to our community. The house where the Staggses lived was about halfway between.

That was after the McKees came there. This was one of the McKees doing a jig, and this was Mrs. Thomas and Colita Schalbar and that was one of the McKee girls. That was Etta Mae and this

*was Ruth. That was the size of her. I can't place this girl . . .
anymore than I can fly to China. That's odd.*

*Les Thomas had a game leg, so he wouldn't dance, but he'd
call the square dancing. Every square he was out there, and he had
more fun than anybody with that game leg.*

In Doris's time, they did not plan a dance weeks in advance
with posters or hire a band to play. Life was more informal.
Somebody would say, "Hey, you all come over to the house
Saturday night, and we'll have a dance." News traveled swiftly,
and everyone soon knew about it.

*When we had the money we'd have oil for a coal oil lamp. If we
didn't, we'd build up a fire in the cook stove. Wood was cheap
because you just went out and cut it anywhere. We'd take the eyes
off the stove and get ready for the party with the fire for light.*

They all would wear the best they had. Doris recalls taking a
coffee can, cutting it into strips, putting paper on the strips and
using them as curlers.

Man, I'd curl my hair.

*One time, Cal or Raggie sent me a gift with a ribbon on it. I
hoarded that ribbon like it was gold and Dorothy and I would take
turns wearing it in our hair at the dance. I would wear it two or
three sets and then she would. We passed that bow around. We
called it our glamour bow. I don't recall even having any makeup.
We sure didn't use it. It was just us. But we had fun.*

Every man, woman, child, and dog would go. Many people came
by wagon. They would throw a mattress in the back so that when
the kids got tired they would have a place to lie down. Doris's family
always walked everywhere, since they did not have a car or even a
wagon in the early days. Often, friends from nearby communities
would join the Caudills in going to a dance and then stay a week
with them after the dance before going home.

*We had a pig named Archie and three dogs—an old one, Pat, that
Faro had brought from Missouri with him, and two younger ones*

we named Laura Bell and Heavy. If anyone drove up in our yard, the dogs, pig, and goat all ran out to meet them. I guess that as I look back now that we were the characters of the community. The pig and the three dogs always went with us when we went to dances or anywhere else. When Mama and Dad came the first time, they brought us a goat and she went with us, too. All the livestock went with you when you went anywhere.

The Divide and Pie Town communities were fortunate in having many local musicians. When everybody got there, there would be two or three guitar pickers and fiddlers. Others played the piano and wind instruments. A couple of musicians played for a while; then they would dance while somebody else played.

Nearly every Saturday night, the Divide community would come together at the largest homes, the Thomases or the Staggses. Both were bigger and more comfortable than the Caudills' one-room dugout with dirt floor and walls plastered with catalog pages. Bill and Odie Staggs, for instance, had come from Oklahoma with enough money to buy a place that had already been proved up by earlier homesteaders. They had a large aboveground log house with wide-plank wood floors and flowered wallpaper, along with log barns and corrals.

The rooms were small, and so, to make room for people to sit, they would set boards between the homemade benches and chairs. Odie Staggs's quilt frame was hoisted up and fastened to the ceiling. Beds ordinarily filled up the living room, but during a dance everything was moved outside except for one bed for the younger children to sleep on. Doris points to the Lee photograph of the little kids asleep on the bed and laughs when she sees it.

That's my Josie. That's her big feet. Bless her heart, she's like her mother. She always had those big feet.

Lee photographed the typical combination of fiddler and guitar at that square dance in June 1940 at the Staggs's home. Seated on two wood chairs in the corner are Olie McKee, Roy's brother, playing the fiddle on his breastbone, and Jimmy Norris playing the guitar. Both have on their best pants and shirts and look solemn in their concentration. Next to them, hunkered down on the floor, is Jimmy's father, Sam Norris, a tie on his neck and a smile on his face as he watches the dancers. Lee has shot the image from floor level so that all that can be seen of the dancers is a pair of heeled shoes, loose-fitting pants, and a bent elbow.

> *One of the most interesting events that I photographed was an evening of square dancing at Bill Staggs's. In one corner the orchestra, consisting of a fiddle and two guitars, was tuning up. Square dances, Paul Jones, broom dances, round dances, individual exhibitions by the women and the men followed in rapid succession. The children slept in the other wing of the house.*
>
> *At midnight there was an intermission for food, cakes, cookies, pies, coffee. Somebody produced two cases of beer—it was rapidly consumed. The party went back to the dance. Bill Staggs forgot his game leg, Adams forgot that he hadn't danced for three years, Les Thomas let himself go. The orchestra played with more pep and zip. The jigging started—it became an informal contest. They were still whooping it up at 4 a.m. when I had to go back to town to change film.[26]*

Olie McKee appears in the famous Lee image of the jig dancer. He had gotten tired playing the fiddle and since there was no music when he quit playing, he danced a jig beating out the rhythm with his feet.

Couples in the 1930s and 1940s did not dance like young people do today, Doris tells me. They danced together, not half way across the room from each other. And they matched their motions to the music. She shakes her head, mystified as to why a simple pleasure like dancing together should have been lost.

Not everybody could dance at the same time. Since the rooms were small, the dancers had to take turns. The musicians would sit in the corner so there would be room for twelve or fourteen couples. But everyone danced who wanted to. The kids joined in, too, as soon as they were old enough to stay up at night. If the boys were hesitant about getting out on the floor, the girls pulled them out. It was a common sight for boys to run out the door with girls chasing after them and bringing them back. The girls danced with each other if there were not enough partners.

If they did not have musicians some evening, they would make up "play-party" games—singing games, broom games, and ring games. Doris remembers one called "Go In and Out the Window," where the men would hold their hands up in a circle and the women slipped in and out under their upraised arms; then each man would grab and swing whoever was closest to him when they stopped singing. If a girl had a special guy she wanted to dance with, she would go real slow and hold up the whole traffic so that she could be right by that guy when they sang, "Swing your partner."

Lee's photographs of the Staggs's square dance that Saturday night in 1940 are the best known of his Pie Town images. His shots of the children sleeping, the musicians playing and the Caudills and their neighbors dancing have been reproduced often. For those like Doris who lived within that time, Lee's photographs have almost come to stand for the experience itself. The vividness of Lee's images has intensified some of their memories, and caused others to fade. Photography is such a robustly detailed visual medium that it can make one forget what is going on outside the picture, or if remembered, make it seem less important. The photographs served to record a memorable evening, and then the photograph became the memory. Those who were there remember that night more than any of the other dances they attended. With no photographs to remind them, they have forgotten many of the details of other dances and events that summer. Because of the power of Lee's photographs, the Staggs's dance has come to stand for many other social activities of the community that he never saw.

Doris was a great dancer, and she and Faro loved to show off. Roy McKee remembers them "dancing up a storm." One evening, Faro in his threadbare best pair of pants got carried away.

One night we were all at a dance, and the end came for the poor old pants. Toy and Billie were there, and they still laugh today about Faro's pants being split wide open. Every time he moved a certain

way his seat flared open like a morning glory, and the cheek of his
backside shone like a new dollar. We didn't know it, however, so
we danced right on . . . having a good time.

About midnight people would break for sandwiches, coffee, and
dessert, then start again. As Doris said, they played as hard as they
worked, often going until morning; then, after breakfast, everybody
would go home to do their chores.

Not all the fun was totally innocent. During the years of Prohibition, dances were a perfect opportunity to distribute the illicit alcohol
that was being manufactured throughout the area. Some of the stills
were large commercial enterprises. Others were simply a way for a
family to make a few dollars. The Caudill homestead, before Fred
Caudill moved in, was the source of some of the local supply. Simon
Potter and his sons occupied the small dugout, by legend one of the
Dalton brothers' hideouts in its earliest days. The Potters stayed
alive by making booze during Prohibition. Nell Potter, Simon's wife,
would come to dances with a pint or half-pint flask taped to the
inside of her calf under her dress. When she sold that one, she would
go out to the wagon and get another. She was not the only one.
Liquor was a natural companion to life on the hard side.

Whiskey could be cheaply made and readily acquired by barter.
Several of the men would get together and raise corn, buy the sugar,
and then sell the liquor in fruit jars, jugs, or flasks. Fred and Faro did
not make it, but they liked to drink and would trade a sack of corn
or a pig for liquor. Everybody had it.

Social decorum mandated that women drink little and that
men drink outside the main social activity. It is still like that in
Catron County:

It's a whole different world out there. The real old cowboy, he may
be a little bit dusty and a little bit dirty and his hair is a little too long
and he hasn't had a bath in a day or two, but you won't find a man
anywhere that treats a woman any better. They will tip their hat. At
a dance they will ask you politely, thank you when the dance is
over, and take you back to wherever they got you, instead of leaving

you in the middle of the dance floor. You don't see any drinking in a public building. They will go outside. (Colita Schalbar)[27]

Russell Lee has a couple of photographs of men with liquor bottles in their hands, but otherwise his camera concentrates, not surprisingly, on the dancing and music of social events.

On 20 June 1940, Lee wrote Stryker that he had completed a good deal of work in Pie Town:

Arrived here this morning from Pietown. Have sent in 21 dozen cut film—and 6 rolls of Contax—you should receive that Monday.

The community sing was really grand and the square dance had one of those fast rhythms with a great deal of abandon. I hope my pix show it.   —Lee to Stryker, 20 June 1940

BACK TO PIE TOWN

I spread the map out on the seat of my car. I am on Doris's trail. I have decided to return to Pie Town after my first meeting with her in Cascade Locks. I am going back in time, back in Doris's life. I am on Lee's trail, too. Along the way I hope to find an imprint of the events and times that brought them both together.

Pie Town is not far from where I live in Santa Fe—a couple of hours drive south through Albuquerque to Socorro, then due west for another couple of hours into the Socorro Mountains and up to the Continental Divide. On a warm September morning, I pick up Highway 60 in Socorro and drive west, past a wrecked car lot, a place to buy cement and cinder block, and the National Guard armory with a watchtower perched on metal legs.

Doris on Blue Dog

The land is open and scrubby. Recent quarrying scars the red sandstone hills. Scattered debris from abandoned mining claims lies about where the vegetation was chopped down decades ago.

Doris traveled this highway with the Mickeys and as a young bride on her two-day honeymoon with Faro on her move away from home. But while she lived at Divide she rarely had transportation for a lengthy trip. Although she had inherited her grandfather's Model T Ford, it was not suitable for distance travel. "We pushed it up the hills so we could ride down," she says. Her economic circumstances fenced her world. Even so, she occasionally found a way to slip out briefly, if only for the twelve-mile trip to Pie Town from Divide:

This picture is me on old Blue Dog, the horse that belonged to Faro. He brought it with him when he moved out, and everywhere he went, he had that horse. After I moved out there I used to ride horseback once a week to town. Going to town meant Pie Town. That was the big city as far as we were concerned. When Josie came, I'd put her up in the saddle in front of me.

My road twists uphill past canyons and arroyos, land where the Apache roamed and hunted for centuries. To my left as I ascend is a small shrine to the Santo Niño de Atocha. I park and walk over. I have to kneel in front of a building no larger than a doghouse in order to open the tiny door and peer in at the lighted candles. A plaster-of-Paris child in his blue gown sits on an ornate chair, and underneath him are hand-written religious postcards, notes, and a crocheted purple cross: offerings to this local patron saint of travelers. I stand back up and look around. Except for an occasional car on the highway three hundred feet away, I see no one and no dwellings, only a roadrunner who stops long enough to look me over. It is so desolate that I feel grateful for this odd but sacred place.

Back on the highway, I pass a couple of cars and three motorcyclists with yellow rain gear. Sunflowers bloom in the ditch. The road kill is all rabbits. In a roadside pullout, two ravens sit on matching fence posts next to a metal garbage can.

When Doris first traveled this road, it was known imposingly as the "Ocean to Ocean" highway. It was less famous than its northern neighbor Highway 66 (Steinbeck opens a chapter of *Grapes of Wrath* with the words, "66 is the path of a people in flight"), but like Highway 66, it carried many Dust Bowlers on their westward migration to California. Despite its pretensions to grandeur, when Doris and the Mickeys came to Pie Town, the highway was well-rutted dirt and a source of constant complaint to anyone who had to travel it. It was narrow, unpaved, and slick as a skating rink when it rained. It was not completely paved until 1957. Today, it is a good paved highway, but it has forgone its aspirations to be an "Ocean to Ocean" highway and settled for rural serenity.

Some twenty-six miles up the road is Magdalena, a town with a wild past. Located in a mineral-rich area, it became a center of silver mining in the 1860s. In 1885, the railroad brought ore out from the smelter, and Magdalena became a railhead for sheep and cattle as well. In June, wool clippings arrived by wagon train. In the spring, large herds of cattle were driven to town along the Magdalena Stock Driveway. When Doris first met Faro, he was working on the driveway, herding cattle. It was a trail that rivaled the Chisolm and Goodnight Trails and outlasted them by dozens of years. More cattle were freighted away from Magdalena by rail than from any other town west of Chicago. With the availability of such prosperous possibilities—and abundant liquor—miners and cowboys led wild and bloody lives. In Magdalena they say that if all the men killed in town were laid end to end, one could walk on dead men all the way from the upper end of the business district to the railway depot at the lower end, 250 yards away.

By the time Doris got to Pie Town, Magdalena had grown less wild. The town had a newspaper, the *Magdalena News,* and several hotels. F. G. Nichols ran the Purity Bakery. Nearby were the Stendel Electrical Works and Moore's Meat Market, the Ocean-to-Ocean Garage and the Antiseptic Barbershop, "the cleanest and best equipped shop in town. Hot or cold tub or shower baths." Supplies came in by rail to the Ilfeld Warehouse, a building that still stands next to the train tracks. The Becker Mactavish Store was a primary supply place for all the ranchers in the area, usually fitting them out with six months worth of supplies. The store even included a bank. Magdalena was the place Pie Towners came for supplies when they could afford to buy in bulk and were able to find transportation for the journey.

Today, the town is sleepy and nearly deserted. The main activity is at Evett's ice-cream store on one corner and the combined Thrifty Mart and post office across the street. I turn right at Evett's and drive a block to a small brick building housing the *Magdalena Mountain Mail,* as it is now called. Jacky Barrington, editor and publisher, hands me a cup of coffee and clears papers off a chair next to her desk for me. The newspaper office is where to come to find out what is going on in the area. Men take off their cowboy or baseball hats as they walk in to ask a question or buy an ad. The phone rings constantly.

Things are changing these days, Jacky tells me. "I only report the news," she says; then she admits she is concerned. Retired folks are moving in with ideas for new small businesses. "Why," she says, "a company from California is starting a Magdalena Seltzer Water Company." Modern American entrepreneurship has arrived on the fringes of the frontier. The newcomers value security and are uneasy with their neighbors, the loners and hippies who have been living in fixed-up school buses around in the hills. For their part, the longtime residents are unhappy with the new zoning restrictions that threaten the freedom of their lifestyle.

Past Magdalena, at an elevation of 6,548 feet, the hills melt slowly down to the plains of St. Augustine, a Pleistocene lake bed. Several thousand years ago these dry and dusty plains were bordered by smoking volcanoes and shimmered with an abundance of fresh water—Lake St. Augustine, some forty-five miles long and fifteen miles wide. Paleo-Indian sites ring the prehistoric lake bed. Excavations indicate habitation by various nomadic groups dating back at least six thousand years, and chronicle the gradual development of agricultural cultivation of corn and squash. In the 1770s, bloody battles were fought on the Plains between Spanish settlers and the Apaches.

Today, the lake bed is a flat open plain ringed with mountains, the sort of uninhabited place an alien culture might well pick for a quiet landing. Cholla and agave dot the grassy bowl along with an occasional scrawny juniper and the blue-green coyote melon gourd vines that are so common along New Mexico highways.

By the nineteenth century, cattle ranchers had won the upper hand over the Apaches, and the Plains became part of their driveway west to Magdalena. Cowboys herded sheep about five miles a day and cattle about ten miles a day, allowing them to graze as they moved. Chuck wagons and extra horses followed behind. The 125-mile driveway was in operation from about 1885 to 1971. During the time Doris lived nearby, the Civilian Conservation Corps fenced the driveway and drilled water wells every ten miles. Although usage declined steadily after the peak year of 1919, Doris was able to see the undulating stream of wide-eyed cattle on several occasions when she came from her homestead into Pie Town.

Today, the cattle are gone, and the only eye-catching shapes are an array of twenty-seven gleaming white antennas that sprout like giant mushrooms from the barren plain. These eerie dish-shaped apparitions are mounted on double railroad tracks stretched in a twenty-mile-long **Y** across the plains. Each dish is eighty-one feet in diameter and weighs 230 tons. Together they form a giant radio telescope, the Very Large Array or VLA, operated under the auspices of the National Science Foundation. The telescope is used by astronomers from around the world to gather data and to take radiophotographs of the sky.

On the far side of the Plains, as I head west, are the Catron County line and the small town of Datil, some fifteen miles east of Pie Town. Sprawled over 7,500 square miles, Catron County has only about two thousand people scattered over the vast landscape like a shake of pepper on a plate. Some ten thousand elk and thirty-four thousand cattle considerably outnumber the locals.

In Doris's day, Datil was home to the Navajo Lodge, a ritzy, two-story log hotel that catered to the whims of summer visitors. I am less fortunate. Datil makes Magdalena look like a bustling metropolis, since it hosts only a small grocery with a couple of gas pumps, restaurant, and small motel, collectively known as the Eagle Guest Ranch.

When I visit Pie Town, I make do with the Eagle Guest Ranch's minimal comforts. The name promises home-cooked barbecue and a stable of willing horses and handsome guides. Neither exists. Each of the eight motel rooms has a distinctive pattern of stains and cracks, and the parking lot is littered with cigarette butts. The shower in my bathroom works but is awkwardly placed only five feet from the ground so that I feel like a giant bathing in a dollhouse.

The café has a weary salad bar to one side of a large room hung with a deer's head, rusty spurs, and framed yellow news clippings. It is the only place to eat dinner for thirty miles in any direction since the Pie Town café only serves a limited menu of soup and grilled sandwiches. To the locals, the Eagle is known for its chicken fried steak and mashed potatoes and gravy. I opt for a bowl of soup. The pies in the glass case to the left of the counter are home-made and look delicious, but I decide to wait for pie until I get to Pie Town.

From Datil to Pie Town, the road climbs again, this time to the Continental Divide at 7,796 feet. The vegetation gradually changes as more and more ponderosa and spruce poke awkwardly out above the low junipers and piñons. Before the logging at the beginning of the century, pine forest enveloped and softened the ragged mountains throughout this high area, but only scattered evidence remains of the existence of large stands of timber.

As I drive into Pie Town, I see a couple of abandoned white buildings that were once service stations. The buildings Doris knew and Lee photographed are nowhere to be seen. Gone are the old post office, the café, the general store, garage, and taxidermy shop. The new Pie Town Post Office was moved from its old location in the mid-1940s when the highway was straightened and is proudly marked not only by its flag but also by two large signs, one over the door and a long hand-lettered one on small posts under the window. In the other half of the same building is a sign for H&R Block, and next to the post office is the building that was the Arch McPhaul store when Doris was here—a long building with the entrance on the end facing the highway. The entrance gate is festooned with junk, ladders, rusty chains, old glass insulators from telephone lines, decrepit tables, and wood and metal scraps of all kinds.

Next to the former store, a metal thunderbird sign says "STOP" in big letters. It was once the namesake for the Thunderbird Trading Post, which has recently been sold to Kathy Knapp from Dallas and renamed the Pie-O-Neer. Kathy and her staff bake all the pies and provide a warm welcome to locals and tourists alike. Her hours vary from season to season, but she is busiest during the summer, when more frequent tourists see the Pie Town road sign and stop for coffee and a piece of pie.

Further on is another service station building that says "Diesel" and "Open," both untrue. The pumps are gone, and the windows of the service bay are cracked and dirty. In the back are restrooms with red and white trim on the outside wall, but the doors hang open on loose hinges.

When Russell Lee was here, he took a few color images that show that all the community buildings were once painted red, white, and blue—the Farm Bureau building, the hardware and feed store, the café and curio shop, the windmill, the storage tank, and even the double outhouse. When I ask Doris whether this was a patriotic gesture, she laughs and says the colored paint came free from Standard Oil. The company had some leftover paint from their highway service station and donated it to the town as free advertising. To save money, the residents painted the town in the company colors. By the time I drive through, only the large shed once used for pinto bean storage retains a few remnants of its original colors.

I pull into a small dusty park just off the highway and stop under the shade of a cottonwood tree near the volunteer fire department station. It is quiet here. An occasional car zooms past on the highway, but the only sign of local life is a pickup truck driven by a tall, rangy man in boots, Levi's, and Stetson who enters the post office on the other side of the highway.

As I approach the neighborhood where Doris lived years ago, I feel surrounded by human absence. Scattered debris from old houses and rusted cars are indications of occupation from a previous time, but where are the current inhabitants? I recall the Very Large Array satellite dishes out on the plains of St. Augustine that I passed not long ago. Driving across that broad bowl was like being on a doomed planet where people once lived but no longer do so. Human technologies were evident in the giant structures, but where were the engineers and scientists who built them? Pie Town and Doris's world has changed irrevocably, irretrievably. The place, and the ghostly remains it harbors, send me into a kind of dream state.

What would it be like to live here today, I wonder? I try to imagine myself living in one of the small frame houses just behind me. Few distractions would intrude. I would live in a quiet way unimaginable to those in a large city. The nearest large grocery is in Socorro, eighty miles away, and more esoteric shopping or medical needs would necessitate a trip to Albuquerque, 170 miles away. Unlike Doris, I could receive regular phone and postal service, even e-mail. I could also get television reception if I could afford a satellite dish, but the nearest theater for seeing a large-screen movie is in Socorro. I would have an even more difficult time than Doris did raising a garden because yearly rainfall has decreased since the thirties, but I could build a small greenhouse with the option of solar panels, and I would have the considerable advantages of electricity, running water, and a telephone. What I would not have is Doris's conviction that if she worked hard enough, she and her family would make a more comfortable life for themselves. That dream is no longer here for the grabbing.

What about my neighbors? Catron County has a prickly reputation around the state. Its residents, primarily ranchers, have led a grass-roots movement in recent years against federal regulation. Ironically, the federal government owns about two-thirds of the county so that the ranchers are in the awkward position of both benefiting from federal subsidies and relief programs and resenting the restrictions the government places on them. Making ends meet in this harsh land is such an uncompromising task that anyone in a position of outside authority is suspect. The locals blame environmentalists, the Forest Service, the Bureau of Land Management, and just about anyone else who visits the county on official business.

I found this out the hard way. Twice on visits to the area men greeted me with rifles in hand as I approached a house to ask for information or directions. Once a rancher forced my car off a dirt road, furious that I had stopped for a moment to look out my car window at an old church on his property. "Don't you respect private property?" he shouted at me. "If you weren't a woman, I'd thrash you."

Another afternoon, I was ordered from a deserted patch of land close to the Divide road where I was trying to find the location depicted in one of Lee's photographs. Although I had crossed no fence and had not seen any No Trespassing signs or any nearby ranch house, I was roughly told by a surly ranch manager with two rifles in his pickup that I was trespassing on private property. My apology and explanations were countered by threats of prosecution, and I quickly left. Private property in Catron County today is sacred, and the days when strangers received a welcome and an offer to join the family at dinner are long past. Not that western chivalry and hospitality are dead; they simply require a proper introduction in Catron County.

Russell and Jean Lee, too, encountered suspicious glances when they first came to Pie Town. Roy McKee told me that when the Lees first arrived, a brief rumor went around that Lee, because of his cameras, was a German spy. For a short time feelings were tense, but then Russell and Jean were introduced at a town meeting and within days "that government fellow" and his wife were welcome at homes throughout the area.

From Pie Town, I must find my way to Divide, Doris's old neighborhood. The community never had a business district or a post office, so no indication of it appears on my New Mexico map. However, during our first meeting in Cascade Locks, Doris drew me a map of how she came from Pie Town to Faro's homestead. Then, with no hesitation, she drew a circle for Alegra Mountain and then the homestead locations and the names of all her neighbors of fifty-five years ago, as if she had left the area the week before. She knew the members of every family. As she drew the map she told me the gossip about each family—who married whose daughter and which children had gone to school with Josie.

We would leave Pie Town and come across these dikes here. A bald eagle made his nest right there all the time. We'd come by the Dahls's ranch; that was sort of half way. Here was where Potters lived with their three girls and Grandma Mickey. This was the Brutons. A man named Jess Bruton came out from Texas. He had some money so he built a log cabin here and put a metal roof on it. Because it had a metal roof, he could put a cistern in the middle of it, and so he didn't have to haul water. When he left and went back to Oklahoma, Mrs. Staggs and her husband bought it.

Eyeing Doris's map, I turn south from Pie Town toward the mountain. I travel a dirt road that is well graded, and though I am not sure I am on the right road, I see no other. Just south of Pie Town the road passes through an opening in a long dike formation. There is no other passage. Doris must have ridden through here on horseback on her way from her homestead to Pie Town whenever she went into town for supplies or to deliver her newspaper column. I am on her trail now.

THE HOMESTEAD

I look at Doris's map and then drive the rutted dirt road south from Pie Town. More than fifty years have passed since Doris was last here, so her map shows me history rather than what I now see. She has drawn a short line indicating the eleven miles from Pie Town to Divide. She was more concerned with where the Brutons and the Potters lived than with the drive out from Pie Town. The road is unmarked, so when I come to forks I choose the path that will take me closer to Alegra Mountain. It is wide, sparse country. In place of trees are wild sunflowers, *chamisa*, and sand sage—the sort of vegetation you see on land that has been severely overgrazed. I see only one ranch house off on a side road in the ten miles I travel and no vehicles. The air is so clear and the land so open that you can see yesterday leaving and tomorrow approaching just down the road. I could spend hours searching, I realize uneasily, and will never locate the Caudill homestead unless I can find someone to show me the way.

Suddenly, at a fork in the dusty road, I see a hand-lettered red and white sign: "Family Reunion," with an arrow pointing to the left. Curious, I turn and follow the road around a curve and over the top of a small hill. I am now on the skirts of Alegra Mountain. Below me as I come over the hill is a cluster of small log buildings. The field beside the buildings is dotted with trailers, trucks, and small RVs. I pull in beside them and park the car. As I open the door, the wind pulls it back on its hinges.

On all sides I see small groups of children playing and running with barking dogs. To one side in a flat patch of dirt, men toss horseshoes with great concentration. They are angular and look and move as if they had been put together by a carpenter who used whatever wood scraps and nails and screws were lying around. But someone else created the few women I see. They are round, plump, wearing flower-pattern dresses and shorts, and carrying trays of food toward the house; most must be already inside, out of the wind.

I walk up to a group of men leaning against the side of the building. They are positioned to avoid the worst of the wind, which is raising clouds of dust from the cleared land. When I explain that I am looking for the Caudill home site, I am introduced to Tracey Lamance, a stocky, ruddy-complexioned man who has organized the reunion. He tells me the home site is nearby and suggests I join the line for lunch before we talk about the Caudills. Gratefully, I push open the screen door and proceed to the tables of barbecued beef, corn, potato salad, mashed potatoes, coleslaw, and rolls. A separate table has peach cobbler, Jell-O, and cake. I fill my glass with sweetened iced tea and head out of the crowded house to find a place to eat.

The wind continues to blow. I take my plate around to the side of the house where it is not quite so bad and find a seat on an old bench with several older men. The man next to me, tall and lanky with a wrinkled face, introduces himself as Sam McKee, Roy McKee's nephew. When I tell him that I am searching for Doris's homestead, he tells me that he appears in some of the Lee photos as a small child and that it was another of his uncles, Olie, who is dancing the jig in that famous image of the series. I tell him what Tracey Lamance told me about the Caudill homestead being nearby, and he nods and laconically offers to take me out there after lunch in his pickup since the property adjoins his own land.

Relaxing and eating sauce-slick smoky beef, we watch the children toss horseshoes while the men take a break for lunch. Our paper plates are balanced on our laps and our hands make a wall around them to try to keep the dust out. When I reach down to get my glass of tea to drink, Sam takes a look, gets up to get some dessert and offers to get me another because I am "making cement in there."

When Sam returns he uses his body to shelter the tea and cobbler from the gusts. Is it often like this, I ask him? "It's nice today," he laughs. He tells me his daughter lives in Albuquerque and does not like to come out here even to visit him. "This country is hard on women," he says. "It's too windy, too dirty, and too cold in the winter."

A few women stuck it out longer than most. Sam points out a small log cabin. Years ago, he says, Aunt Lizzie, Faro's aunt and stepmother, used to live there after she separated from Faro's dad. It now adjoins the more modern Lamance house and is being used by them as a guesthouse. I look at it and am astounded. I am eating barbecue in Doris's old neighborhood. Aunt Lizzie's place is clearly marked on Doris's map, and she has indicated that her own is not far away. Seeing this house makes me wonder if there is some trace of Doris's old dugout, too.

I am so close now I feel like Doris might appear at any moment. If she still lived on her homestead, she would walk over for lunch. By evening she would have made friends with just about everyone and been able to tell a story about each person's life. From the map she gave me, I can see that her homestead was less than a section away from where I sit eating cobbler.

After a cup of coffee, I climb in Sam's pickup, and we set off going eastward on an eroded track. It is a dry windy mid-day. Too much light and dust have shut down my senses, but I feel I am in good hands. Every so often Sam stops, and I get out to open and close a gate. The land here at the base of the mountain is hilly, and the road is rutted and rough going. Sam tells me that his own house is on ten acres that were once part of the Caudill homestead, but that the Caudill dugout is now on the property adjacent to his, which is being leased for grazing by Tommy Padilla, the brand inspector for Catron County. We drive slowly to dodge rabbitbrush that has grown up in the narrow tracks, across a large arroyo, and out into an open meadow of grama grass and then up a slight hill. A scrawny jackrabbit hops out from behind a bush and stops. Instead of running away at the sound of our arrival, it stands motionless and looks hopeful.

Faro filed the homestead claim on this section, half a mile wide and two miles long, Doris told me. When his father and Aunt Lizzie married and moved to Divide, she had the money to buy one of the few proved-up homesteads. Even though Lizzie was married to Fred, she put the deed for her place in the name of her three boys. Aunt Lizzie was like that; she watched out for herself and her own kids. That left Pop, Faro, and Loraine without any property of their own. So Faro went over and filed his own claim on an adjacent section.

The Caudill dugout
Photo: Joan Myers

After Pop and Aunt Lizzie separated, Faro and his father and sister moved to an abandoned dugout and house on Faro's claim.

Today, sixty-five years later, I approach this homestead where Doris first lived when she and Faro married and she moved to Divide. I climb through a barbed wire fence with Sam and stand on a low hill. The site is on the west side of a great draw. At one time this area, too, must have been forested, but it was cleared for bean fields and today the vegetation is minimal, mainly grama grass, rabbitbrush, snakeweed, and turkey peas. Across the draw are a few low hills, one with a rocky outcropping that Doris used to climb.

Below me is an open meadow. Beyond, the view is a long one, across the meadow that Doris talked of having cleared for beans, and off in the distance to the Sawtooth Mountains. Some eleven miles away are the roofs of Pie Town. Behind and overhead is Alegra Mountain. To one side on the slight decline is a small stand of ponderosa and juniper with a few posts sticking out of the ground and small piles of sun-bleached lumber.

I still have Doris's map showing the location of her three different homestead dugouts: Pop Caudill's place, where I stand and she and Faro lived for over a year, the site with the double ridgepole that Lee photographed and where they lived for six years, and the final site with water where they lived for a couple of years before moving to Albuquerque. All three sites are located along a broad sandy draw in their section homestead.

As I walk down to Pop Caudill's place, I recall Lee photographs of the area—images of the simple dugouts and houses, of Faro working to clear the land, of Doris ironing inside her dugout. Overlaid on the remembered images I see the unphotographable ambience that Lee also saw but could not include: the colors, the midday heat, and the sound of flies.

Interwoven is the infinite richness of time and lives that used to be.

A hand-hewn water trough, its wood rotting, sprawls out across the dirt. Rabbitbrush grows up where milk cows used to graze. On the hill behind the water trough are the remains of an old corral and a small barn built of machine-milled lumber. A stone chimney is all that remains from the one-room house where Doris and her family, before the open fire, read the hometown newspapers her mother sent them.

Inside dugout
Photo: Joan Myers

Behind the house, set into the side of the hill, is the original Pop Caudill family dugout where Doris cooked for several years after she married Faro and before they were able to build their own dugout a mile further up the draw.

Pop Caudill's dugout is in remarkably good condition. Three sides of the dugout are sunk into the side of the hill, and the fourth side with the doorway faces out toward the open draw below. The walls are made of unpeeled ponderosa logs set on a foundation of large flat rocks; the size of the logs must have insulated the family well against the summer heat and winter cold. The construction is rough and functional with the broad gaps between the logs still chinked with mud. When I duck in the doorway, I see scraps of the mud-plastered strips of handmade wood lath that must have completely covered the inside walls. The roof above the ridgepole was originally formed of horizontal poles first covered with rabbit-brush and then eight to ten inches of dirt. Some of the roof still remains, but most of the dirt has fallen into the dugout. When Doris lived here, the floor was dug four feet down below ground level, but now the fallen roof has raised the height of the floor almost to the level of the outside land. Sam tells me it is called a half-dugout since it was dug half into the ground and built half above.

I go back outside and poke around behind the dugout. The ground is covered with scraps of wood, nails, tin cans, purple glass, and bits of china with flowers. A small grayish-brown lizard zips out from under a board and stands in the sun watching me set up my view camera. Lee never photographed Pop Caudill's dugout because Doris and Faro had already moved by the time he arrived. He did, however, make one of his few landscape long shots from close to where I set up my camera. Although the homestead buildings are not visible in Lee's image, you can see some of the Caudill pasture, a fence, and the Sawtooth Mountains in the distance.

Next to the dugout are the wood chip remains of a small house also built of vertical logs. The fireplace was made of volcanic native stone, but most of it has fallen down. Another pile of rubble nearby I recognize from Doris's descriptions as the remains of a storage shed.

> There was one big room with a fireplace and an unfinished half dugout with a dirt floor where there was a table and a stove. We moved our bed in the big room with Pop and Loraine. I put my dishes and pots and pans and such on some wooden crates that I made into cabinets in the half dugout. It didn't have any floor to it. That's where I cooked and everything. Right in front of the stove was a great big rock the size of my head. One day when my brother came to see me, he said, "I'm tired of you stubbing your toe over that rock. I'm going to get that out of there." So he went out and got Faro's axe and he started breaking up that rock. He broke it up and carried it outside, so I didn't have that anymore. When he came, he took this picture.

Several months after my first visit with Sam McKee, I return to Divide. This time I come alone. I want to get a sense of the land without a tour guide. I want to photograph without distractions or interruptions. Once again I return to Pop Caudill's homestead, the place Doris and Faro lived when they were first married.

Sand sage grows along the pickup ruts that I follow as I drive in, and I can smell it on my car's warm underbelly when I stop. It is a July morning, and as I walk around the remains of the old dugout and house, the dryness crinkles my skin and the inside of my nostrils. Average annual precipitation in Pie Town is only about twelve inches, including snowfall. When I reach down and pick up a handful of dirt, it is so dry that it runs through my fingers like sand. In other places it is so hard that I cannot scratch it off with my fingernail.

Anthills are everywhere. I cannot sit down on the ground to load film without being covered with an ant swarm. They are small black ones and though they do not bite hard, their curse is in their numbers. What if they get in my camera when I change film?

A scatter of cow bones reminds me of my young son's question years before when he first encountered similar bones: "Mommy, if we just get all the bones, can we make a cow?" In Cascade Locks, when Doris told me that water was always her most prized possession when she lived in Pie Town, her words seemed like an exaggeration. Standing here, I can feel my skin shriveling, and looking at these bleached remains, I understand that she meant it.

This is a picture of me in front of Pop's dugout not too long after we got married. Here was Pop's place and the windmill . . . and this was a big field, and at the top of the field was where Faro built our own homestead, closer to the school.

After Doris and Faro married and found themselves financially obliged to move in here with Pop and Loraine, they began immediately to clear land for their own dugout along the same sandy draw about one mile to the north. It was a lengthy and laborious process that Faro completed just before Josie was born.

This is our place. Faro built a half dugout that was fourteen-by-twenty-eight. I helped him. He grubbed the rabbitbrush, and I grubbed, too. What I couldn't do was heavy trees.

When I moved there, there was just a patch of yard and a garden spot and a field, but it wasn't too big. The homestead was *half a mile wide and two miles long. The government gave the 640 acres to anybody who would go and live on it and "prove up." You had to put a certain amount of improvements like a livable house and a fence and clear so much land. They set the standards of so many miles of fence was worth so much and a house was worth so much and you had to have I think $500 of improvements on it. You could "prove up" in three years or five years. We chose the five years because that was two years that we didn't have to pay tax on it.*

There was a great big ridgepole in that house, and Doris told me a story about it:

One night I woke up and I could hear something. I thought it was a pack rat. Pretty soon it sounded like that again. Two or three times during the night I heard it, and just before daylight we heard this crack. I got up too see what was going on, and I discovered that the ridgepole was breaking. I called Faro. He run out and cut a sapling to put under the break to strengthen it. and we started walking to Billie's in pouring-down rain. We got over there just as they were getting up. I told them a porcupine had come in the house the night before and gnawed the ridgepole in two and our roof was caving in on us. I was hungry, so we ate breakfast. Then Faro and Bill went around to the neighbors, Mr. Saunders, Harvey, Pop, and several others, and they went down to the dugout and started taking the roof off. We had to remove the ridgepole, and we put in two of them. We put trash on top of them and then bobbed the roof with mud. That kept it from leaking. It took three days, and during that time, wouldn't you know it, it rained day and night.

This is the dugout where Lee photographed Doris patching clothes, milking, and sitting with her family. Lee described his own arrival at this dugout and his initial meeting with the Caudills in his 1941 *U.S. Camera* article:

Armed with a crude map, I put the cameras in the car and drove into the country in the general direction of one of the farmers. The lighting happened to be good for some general long shots of the terrain and countryside so I took a few pictures. As I was driving down one side road, I noticed a farmer and his horse, resting from plowing his field, and looking in my direction. I stopped the car, waved to him; he waved back and I walked across the partially plowed field and introduced myself.

He was a young man, about thirty, named Faro Caudill—a homesteader. We talked together a few minutes among the beans and corn, main crops of the community. He indicated to me the boundaries of his land and pointed out L'Alegra—a mountain of eleven thousand feet rising three thousand feet above the surrounding country. He told me that the Spaniards some three hundred years ago had come through this section and named it L'Alegra—meaning "happy mountains." We walked across the field to meet his wife and daughter. Mrs. Caudill was a tall Texas girl a few years his junior. Josie, their little girl, was a very pert and pretty five-year-old.

We walked down the half dozen steps into the dugout home. It was pleasantly cool—quite a contrast to the warm June day outside. The dugout had been made by excavating a space about five feet deep, fifteen feet wide and thirty feet long. On the ground outside, timbers had been laid to raise the height of the resulting rooms to about nine feet and to provide a place for windows. The roof was of piñon poles covered with dirt intermixed with branches of the piñon. The two rooms were papered with heavy brown wrapping paper and paper from magazines. The furniture showed the sign of long usage but we were comfortable as we sat talking.[29]

In Lee's shots of the dugout exterior, the two ridgepoles are clearly visible. In one shot, Doris is unloading possessions from the rear of an inconstant Model T Ford pickup they had acquired from a neighbor in trade for some lumber he cut on their property. A picket fence has been built to the rear of the dugout. Small objects and scraps of fabric are scattered on the ground. Not a scrap of vegetation remains between Lee's vantage point and the front steps of the structure. After my windblown lunch at the Lamance reunion some months before, I wonder how Doris did her laundry and kept the wind and dirt out of her home.

You can also see from the photograph what Sam meant by "half dugout." A cavity, fourteen-by-twenty-eight-feet long, was dug about four feet down into the earth, and then logs were laid in to raise the roof about four feet above ground level. Inside, Doris divided the space into a sleeping and a cooking area with a wall made from smoothed-out cardboard boxes that reached from the floor up to the ridgepoles. Over the top of the dugout was a sod roof over poles. In the picture you can see the stairs where Doris, Faro, and Josie climbed down into the dugout. Not visible in the picture are the two windows, one on each side. They did not have any money for glass so in the summer the openings were left open to let in air and breezes, and in the winter they were stuffed with newspapers and an old tarp.

Inside, they had few possessions. There was a simple table, and benches that Faro made out of rough lumber from the sawmill, as well as oil-cloth-covered shelving and the stove. Lee photographed Doris ironing in this dugout. Simple pans and crockery line the shelving behind her. She uses a small, heavy iron, one of three she has heating under a skillet on the cookstove. She had one handle and would just move it from iron to iron as one cooled. A pine board covered with cloth served as the ironing board.

From Pop Caudill's dugout I set off on foot up the treeless draw to locate this second site, the place where the young couple finally had a home of their own. It is a long mile away, a hot twenty-minute walk under a cloudless sky. I realize midway that I have no water with me. I would prefer to continue but already I can feel how dehydrated I am and reluctantly I return to my car, drink a can of coke in one long gulp, and then set off again with water bottle in hand. I cannot seem to drink enough liquid.

This time, thanks to Doris's map, I walk straight to the home site, even though there are no standing markers or structures. Even the fencing is mainly gone. Doris tells me that when they found water in between their place and Pop's they moved everything they could, including the wood from the dugout to the site with water. All that remains of this second site are two small depressions, a large one that was the half-dugout and a smaller one that once served as a cellar for Doris's canned goods. In front of the two depressions is a large open area where Doris and Faro grubbed rabbitbrush and then planted beans. Their backbreaking work was unending since new rabbitbrush would spring up each year. Today, the bean plants are only a memory; the rabbitbrush, its buds about to open into bright yellow flowers, reigns supreme.

It is quiet here and far from present-day human activities. Along with scraps of wood and metal on the ground, I find an inch-wide mother-of-pearl button with a double hole in the center. It is a simple flared shape, and I can imagine it on one of Doris's few party dresses. Occasional airplanes whir overhead, but there are no other sounds like cars or voices. Insects chirp and a few birds call out. I hear what Doris heard. The wind bends pine boughs and ruffles the needles. It is a constant noise, ebbing and flowing like the ocean. When I hold up my water bottle, the breeze blows across the opening and makes a singing sound.

It is a pretty site, Doris and Faro's first home of their own, nestled under the flanks of Alegra Mountain. More wooded than the other homesteads in the area, it is isolated and yet protected by the spirit of the mountain. Pine needles, *chamisa*, and dry earth perfume the air around me. I can easily imagine Josie dashing up behind it into the ponderosa timber, gathering piñon sap for gum, or climbing part way up the mountain. If you look down the draw you cannot quite see Pop's place, but you can see a road that goes over to the Divide schoolhouse where Josie went to school and where the Literary Society met. This school, with its hardwood floor and little stage, was so well built by the community that it is still standing, along with the tiny teacherage behind it.

A little farther north on the far side of the draw, midway between Pop Caudill's dugout and the one I have just located, is where Doris and Faro moved in 1940. After eight years of dowsing and searching, the Caudills finally found water on their homestead.

WITCHING FOR WATER

One thing we'll never ever live down . . . One day when Grandma and Grandpa Beeson and Ozella Fowler and their five kids drove up in their car, Josie was out in the yard. She was busy making mud pies or something. She was maybe three years old. Since she didn't have any water to make clay, she just squatted down and wet the mud, and then she just got up. They were setting there in the car watching, and they tell that on Josie, and they just got the biggest kick out of that you ever saw.

Of course, none of Doris and Faro's neighbors had running water or indoor plumbing. Like the Caudills, most people did not even have a well since it was so hard to find water. They had to carry in or cart in all the water they used. Sam McKee says that even if you struck water, you did not find much of it.

For a well around here, you can expect a gallon a minute. Two gallons a minute here is a good well. I get half a gallon here but I had to drill five holes to find it. I'm down twenty-six feet right here at the corner of the barn. Now out there I have a 200-foot hole that's dry. If you miss it by six inches you won't get nothing.

The shortage of water was an acute problem for the Divide community. In Pie Town in the early days, local settlers could drive into town and pump and haul water from a well, since dried up, at the Keele store. That was too far for those in the Divide community to travel to haul water. Few of them even had automobile transportation. They were dependent on a few local wells of poor quality.

Farming here was always dryland farming without irrigation of any sort. Success in growing enough to eat was a crapshoot. The necessary snow and rain depended on the whim of the local weather gods that particular spring and summer. Doris and Faro always

Corner of dugout
Photo: Joan Myers

struggled just to grow what they needed for the family to eat. If enough rain came, they would also try to grow pinto beans and maize for cash crops.

Roy McKee, Sam's uncle, grew pinto beans for a number of years after he arrived in the late thirties, a thousand sacks of them one year. "I thought I could do that every year," he told me, but as time when on, he found farming to be less and less profitable. Weather patterns changed, and even dryland farming was impossible by the late 1950s because of less precipitation. Not easily discouraged, however, he took advantage of his neighbors' need for water, acquired an old well machine, and began drilling. Starting in 1955, Roy drilled wells from Magdalena to the Arizona line for twenty-two years. He drilled the first wells in Pie Town. Even today, the town gets its water from two wells on his land that he drilled in 1963 and gave to the town. "There's not enough water up in Pie Town to water the chickens," he tells me. The galvanized pipes he installed in 1963 were good for almost thirty years and were finally replaced by PVC pipe in 1991.

For Doris and Faro, not having a well meant year-round physical labor more typical of life in an African village than twentieth-century America. One of Doris's snapshots shows Faro with Aunt Lizzie's wagon. In order to get water in those early days, Faro had to go down to Pop's, borrow a team of horses, and then walk up to Aunt Lizzie's and borrow a wagon, and drive five or six miles past their neighbor Granny Johnson's place, almost halfway up to the highway. At the windmill there, he would use buckets to fill the containers on the wagon. He then brought the water home, returned the wagon to his aunt and the horses to his father, and walked home. He would do that twice a week.

Lee also photographed Faro with Aunt Lizzie's wagon. He is drawing water from the well using a pulley-wheel mechanism and

filling large metal milk containers. Next to him are two horses rigged
to pull a wooden sleigh-like wagon. His father, Fred, sits quietly on
the back of the wagon, his hands in his lap, his face shadowed by
his broad hat.

For the first nine summers they lived there, Faro hauled all their
water. It was an unending and laborious necessity. In the winter
Doris took over:

> *In the wintertime, as soon as the first snow fell, I started melting
> snow for water. That was an endless job. If you think it's not, try to
> melt enough snow. But, it relieved Faro of the water hauling.*

Several of Lee's photos show Pop Caudill with a dowsing stick
witching for water, a process both mystical and practical that
continues to this day in rural New Mexico. The dowser holds a
forked stick in both hands and walks out over the land. When water
is to be found, the stick twists and points downward. It is not uncom-
mon today in the arid West for a landowner to hire both a dowser and
a water engineer to survey his land before determining where to drill

a well. Jean Lee tells me she tried
dowsing while Russell was photographing Pop and that she could feel
the stick twitch in her hands.

Since the site where Doris and
Faro found water was half a mile or
so from where they were living,
they decided to move their home
closer to the water so they would
no longer have to haul their daily
supply. Russell Lee documented this
process. A series of photographs
show the dismantling of the old

Homemade door latch
Photo: Joan Myers

dugout and the site preparation for the new home. The first step
was for Faro to clear the land around the new well with a team of
donkeys. Lee has stooped down in front of the team to show Faro,
cigarette hanging from his mouth, in his checked shirt, overalls and
brimmed hat, holding the plow between the donkeys. Another

image shows Faro with his neighbor, John Adams, who is helping him. They have a large rectangular hole cut in the ground some four feet deep, and Faro is using three donkeys to move the large peeled logs into position for the upper walls.

> *Just before we left, we got water down at the end of the field. We kept clearing and clearing, and about halfway in between Pop's house and our present dugout was where we finally found water. We moved the dugout . . . not the dugout, but the roof and everything. While we were getting a new place to live, we lived in this tent. I cooked on the stove outside or the campfire or wherever I could. That was Josie and I getting ready to go to Sunday school one morning. We walked up the hill to the school building for church. We slept in the tent while we were working on the homestead. It was in 1940 when Lee was taking the photographs.*

I show Doris images that Lee took of the tent they lived in while the new dugout was being built. Doris points out the towel in the picture. She was careful to hang it over the wash pan rather than over the water bucket because she did not want Faro and Josie dripping their dirty hands into the water bucket.

In one image, Doris and Josie are just coming out the open flap of the tent. Doris squints in the bright sun, and Josie wears a bonnet. They both have dresses and shoes on as they leave for church. Several roughly made pine benches are scattered in front of the tent—they did not have any chairs, Doris says. The large black cookstove with a kettle and several pots sits to one side. Its vent pipe rises uselessly, comically upward, venting cooking fumes into the open sky and mimicking the vertical lines of the picket fence behind and the large wood tent stakes.

Now, thousands of miles from Cascade Locks and once again in the Divide area, I pick up my camera and tripod and walk down to the Caudill's third home site. The remnants of the windmill scaffolding lie jumbled together with rabbitbrush a few yards away from where the dugout was once located. The dugout is gone, but its indentation in the earth, as well as the remains of a wood house moved to the location by the subsequent owners, are clearly visible. I have no doubt of the location since the depression in the ground lines up perfectly with the location of the hole being dug in the Lee photo and the hogback mountain behind it.

I set up to photograph, and just as I open the view camera, a dust devil whirls through without warning. It seems too hot for so much activity. One moment it is still, and the next, pine needles, dirt, and cow pies spin through the air like dervishes. I try to cover the camera with the dark cloth and to pull the rear door of the car down, but the wind blows too hard. I can only cover my face and wait for the wind to move on. Dirt flies into my car, camera cases, and clothes. I feel it in my hair and clothes, and taste it as well.

But I do not have to live with the dirt and wind like Doris did. Without giving it much thought, I can shower in the motel when I get done working.

I'd go back to Pie Town but under different circumstances. It would be with being able to have a house and electricity and running water. As old as I am, I like to take a bath now and then. We would take a bath on Saturday night. We had a number three bathtub. I'd get the water all hot and then I'd bathe Josie and then I'd take a bath and then Faro would take a bath. Then I saved it to scrub the floor with, and after we scrubbed the floor, I'd put it on the flower bed. You kind of wore the water out.

THE DREAM ENDS

It took Doris and Faro five years, but they finally completed the necessary improvements and "proved up" on their section. She still has the deed, a yellowing curled sheet of heavy paper signed by Franklin Roosevelt. I hear the pride in her voice as she shows it to me.

But the family continued to struggle. Daily life did not ever get easier, even though they were relieved finally to have their own well and not to haul water. They enjoyed dances, picnics, church socials, and other community social events but they were unable to get ahead financially.

Faro always returned thanks for all except about the last year we lived there. I tried to get him to keep on, but he said he was too mean. I told him we could always be thankful to God for all our blessings, especially our food, regardless of how mean we were otherwise.

Then Faro, always a smoker, began to have lung trouble and had pneumonia most of the winter. That was hard for Doris, too, since she had all his chores to do in addition to her own.

He would be so sick that he would talk out of his head . . . and no doctor for ninety miles. I would doctor him with hot fried onion poultices just as hot as he could stand. He wouldn't feel like getting wood. I used to go out in the snow and drag up as big a branch as I could manage and cut the firewood for our stove. When some of the neighbor men came by, they would cut me a wood box full.

In 1942, Doris reluctantly agreed with Faro's desire to move to Albuquerque so he could get paying work. Because of the war buildup, a lot of defense jobs were available in the larger cities of New Mexico. Pop already had moved down to Socorro, and Faro's sister Loraine had married Ben Burns and moved to a ranch north of Pie Town.

When they left, Faro and Doris sold their place to Granny and Jo Beeson (who appear in several Lee photos). Doris does not remember how much they got for their place, but it seemed all right at the time. Most people who sold out got about a dollar an acre.

Josie, Doris, and Faro in Albuquerque, ca. 1950

I'm sure it wasn't very much because they didn't have too much. They were just like the rest of us.

The Caudills were not the only ones to leave. Most of their neighbors did, too. Like Faro, they went to Albuquerque or on to the West Coast. Olie McKee, the dancer in Lee's famous jigger photograph, moved to California and got a job at Lockheed. Of the "newcomers" who came in the late 1930s from Texas and Oklahoma and bought "proved up" homesteads from those who were leaving, most, except for a few families like the McKees and the Huttons, stayed a few years and moved on. Few ever returned. Their leaving belied the comfortable image of self-sufficiency projected in Lee's photographs. The truth was that neither the Caudills nor their neighbors could make the American Dream come true in Pie Town.

Faro left Doris with the seven milk cows they had accumulated during their stay and went down to Albuquerque hunting work. Eventually, he got a job at the railroad loading dock and came for them. They moved to Armijo, a few miles south of Albuquerque. Here, Doris would milk the cows and then walk to town and work in a local café. She did not know anything about waiting tables, but the café owner was desperate for help and she needed the money.

For Faro, having steady work was a relief. He wrote on his gate when he left: "Farewell, old homestead. I bid you adieu. I may go to hell but I'll never come back to you."

Faro went to work on a loading dock, loading and unloading freight from big trucks and trailers. That was when they were shipping all this equipment up to Los Alamos before that atomic thing. We didn't know what Los Alamos was then. Freight would come in and it would be labeled "egg cartons" or something like that, and it would be real heavy. The men would know it was something different.

I was really sorry to leave . . . and homesick. . . . When we were there in Socorro I was so homesick. I missed my friends so much. I just missed everything.

Eventually, the marriage broke apart. For a time, Doris worked for the Hilton Hotel. Then she found a job working for Empire Craft selling Avon products and eventually hired, trained, and managed salesgirls all over the state. For Doris it was an opportunity she had never even imagined. In a few years she had 165 girls working for her and was bringing home a steady $750-$1000 a month, an amazing income for the time. Faro, working for the Teamsters on the loading docks, was lucky to make $100 a week. She and Faro were each so involved with their work, they were rarely home at the same time and no longer worked together to make a life. The inequality of income and their different schedules and needs were suddenly a story of the twentieth century rather than the nineteenth. Homesteading had been simpler. They had not depended on income or material possessions because they had nothing. They had simply needed each other and shared what they had.

The Belgums, who bought the Caudill homestead

Faro went a little crazy when he got to Albuquerque, she tells me. "They say that men are into wine, women, and song. Well, Faro didn't drink and he couldn't carry a tune . . ."

Her voice trails off, and I sense how difficult it was for her. She does not want to talk about it. It is only the good times she wants to talk about. When things do not work out, they go over, Doris says, "like a cement cloud." Months after our first meeting in Cascade Locks and after the death of her husband Jack, Doris tells me that the divorce from Faro was even harder than death. The wounds festered and stayed open longer.

But she was still young, and before long she set out again.

I went up to Alaska. I was dashing, gay, and young, you know, footloose and "fanny-free." I had always wanted to go to Alaska. In fact, when Faro and I was living on the homestead, and those people from the Kansas Dust Bowl . . . the government subsidized them to go to Alaska to the Matanuska Valley . . . and I just begged Faro to let's go. I always wanted to go. Well, he didn't have the spirit like I wanted, the pioneer spirit.

So, when I got to where I was footloose, I went. I didn't know a soul. My two sisters from Sweetwater came out. They tried to boss me all my life, but I'd just smile and go exactly where I wanted to anyway. Kid, if they could have, they would have had me committed. They felt I was crazy, because I didn't know a soul and I didn't have a job. I was up there for a while and I met Jack. I fell for that big old moose. We have been married thirty-nine years.

*Doris and second
husband in Oregon*

She and Jack filed on a homestead. She has a color snapshot of the two of them smiling and pounding in one of the corner stakes, but they never proved up on it.

That was about twenty miles out of Anchorage on the railroad going up to Fairbanks. You had to ride the railroad up because there wasn't any roads in there. They'd slow down and you'd just jump off. I said, you know, Jack, I served my apprenticeship on a homestead in New Mexico. If you want to go out there and homestead I'll come and see you on the weekends and I'll bring you beans, but I'll stay in town and work and you can go homestead. I'd had enough of homesteading.

All her life she has stared at the empty space caused by divorce, death, or illness, cried a little, and then found the strength to move on. Now, several years after our first meeting in Cascade Locks, she is a widow and alone once again. She puts on a brave front for a moment and asks me if I would like to go to Australia with her. Then she leans back in her chair and falls silent for a long moment. Today it is more difficult, she tells me. "When you get to my age, you don't dare buy any green bananas. You might not be around for them to ripen."

She struggles against increasingly poor eyesight that makes it difficult for her to drive. Her breathing is labored. The specter of another stroke is always with her. After Jack's death, she worries about money. "If it gets much worse," she tells me, "I'll be pickin' with the chickens. When you've done for yourself all your life, it is real hard."

In America we make no mention of failure. Yet, the efforts of the Pie Town homesteaders of the 1930s and 1940s, as documented so positively by Russell Lee, were futile. The idea of planting a garden, milking a few cows, and thereby making a life for their families on a section of arid land did not square with reality. Eventually they had no choice but to leave.

Doris
Photo: Joan Myers

The land was hard on everybody who homesteaded. Sam McKee's remark keeps coming back to me: He said his daughter moved to Albuquerque because the land around Pie Town was so hard on women. He was right in what he said, but he did not go far enough. It was just harder on women. Doris was lucky to get away before the winds and dirt wore her down like the balding rubber tires of their Model T.

Doris's daughter Josie has a unique view of the Pie Town years. While she lived there, from shortly after her birth for almost ten years, she knew no other existence. As a young child, it did not occur to her to wonder if life might have been easier somewhere else. Now, however, more than half a century later, she looks at the Lee photographs as an adult.

You know I really have mixed feelings about the Pie Town pictures. My parents were happy. They had a special friendship with all of the people there. They had something money cannot buy. They needed each other and were willing to share all they had. They all helped one another without expecting something in return. But, Joan, I want to cry and cry when I see the conditions in which they lived. It depresses me greatly.[29]

Josie
Photo: Joan Myers

She questions the experience in a way Doris does not. She finds the images painful for their depiction of a time of suffering for her parents. Although what she can remember from her childhood is pleasant enough, she also remembers the wind and the dirt and the dryness and the unending labor. She remembers enough to be able to feel, in a visceral, very private way, the harshness of the experience that Doris and Faro lived.

For the rest of the country, which first saw the images in the 1941 *U.S. Camera* article, the photographs were uplifting. People were looking for hopeful signs in a time of despair. Lee's widow Jean thinks back over those times:

This country is amazing. We were on the edge of revolution. This country didn't give up. People during the hardest times worked together. Great courage, but they didn't think of it in terms of courage. Just, "times are rough. We'll live through it and help each other."

The Pie Town photographs are important in that they really show the spirit of the American people when they are in trouble. This is quite a country. The photographs show some of the reasons. We built it in worse hardships than that. It wasn't easy to build this country. It was hard physical work.

In his *U.S. Camera* article, Lee, with Jean's uncredited assistance, combined his photographs with an explanatory text. A comment by Faro Caudill is quoted to show the spirit of the homesteaders at a moment of trial:

> *The advertisements used to say nature in the raw is seldom*
> *mild and they must have been talking about homesteading because*
> *it isn't an easy life we've got here—our growing season's short. I've*
> *got to get my seed in the ground the day we're clear of frost (which*
> *is usually the last day of May) or else when the frosts come again in*
> *October my beans won't be matured for the harvest. . . . We came*
> *without money, we've had to grub and clear our own land, dig our*
> *wells, build our corrals and barns as well as our houses. But we*
> *don't go hungry, that's one thing. We raise our own meat and this*
> *land sure grows garden stuff. Doris cans enough to last the winter*
> *through. Not that she's doing anything extra, all the women do.*[30]

Combined with Lee's photos, the statement is powerful story-telling. Faro acknowledges the family's hard work, but he says that the effort has led to bountiful harvests. Faro's comment fits perfectly with the FSA agenda of showing Congress and the American people images of ordinary Americans making a go on their own farm and "off the dole." A casual reader might well infer that the Caudills' home-steading had made them self-sufficient and that FSA programs were responsible for that success. Never mind that it was the Department of Agriculture that was promoting the mechanization and indus-trialization of farming and making homesteading and small family farms unprofitable. The upbeat message of Faro's statement reinforces Lee's images of Faro building his new dugout and inspires the reader with a message whose believability the Depression and Dust Bowl had tarnished: If you work hard, you are bound to succeed.

Perhaps Faro was simply putting on a good front for the Lees, but in any case, he speaks after the fashion of a good photograph. The comment, "This land sure grows garden stuff," is evocative of a well-filled table—like the heavily laden table in Lee's photograph of a portly woman in a flowered dress and apron preparing for a large meal. Jean Lee's caption for this image reads, "Mrs. Bill Staggs, homesteader's wife, putting the coffee on the table for dinner, which consisted of home-cured ham and gravy, pinto beans, corn, homemade pickles, home-grown tomatoes, homemade bread and hot biscuits, fruit salad, cake, two kinds of pie, milk, and coffee."

But reality was more complicated than Lee's captioned photograph suggests. When I show Lee's photograph to Doris, she tells me that it was indeed a scrumptious meal but that it was hardly representative of what they ate. She was there that day, she says. Indeed, the entire community had come to the Staggs's house to help harvest beans. The reason that table was so full of pies, mashed potatoes, and other good food, she says, is that everyone in the neighborhood who had come to help had also brought a dish for dinner. It was not their typical meal of beans, greens, cornbread, and gravy.

The Pie Town photographs describe the community with such an abundance of details that they project a convincing appearance of verisimilitude, but as a matter of fact the Lees colluded with Stryker in a manufactured reality as convincing as a Hollywood drama and just as false. The photographs were not simple documents encouraging knowledge for the sake of democracy, despite Lee's ingenuous comment to his subjects, "I want to show people in other parts of the country how you live. . . . I am a photographer hired by a democratic government to take pictures of its land and its people." Rather, they had a message designed to fit a very particular moment in American history.

Lee's images of a homesteading community were reassuring in a time of poverty, unemployment, and major deprivation. Even though open country free for the taking had disappeared in the early twentieth century, Americans still carried the hope that they were a chosen people specially endowed by their Creator to colonize a new world. For the Lees and Stryker, as well as for the public that eventually saw the magazine images of Pie Town, Doris and Faro replayed the American myth of civilizing the wilderness. Life in Pie Town was a throwback to life on the nineteenth-century western frontier. As Lee put it in the last sentence of his *U.S. Camera* article, "For Pie Town is an authentic incident that proves the American tradition is as alive today as it was one hundred years ago."[31] Part of the reason that Lee's photographs remain so memorable today is because the moment they recorded was a reminder of the defining drama of American history.

Jean Lee explained the need for the photographs:

If you use the word propaganda in its proper use, which is to influ-
ence people in their thinking and actions, that's what these pictures
were about. That's what we were interested in. They were used by
newspapers and magazines and all sorts of places because they
were very good photographs . . . which is exactly what we wanted
them to do, to use them so that people would see them.

Despite their portrayal of suffering and deprivation, Lee's photographs reassure the viewer rather than question the American
Dream. Lee, like Stryker, wanted to see the Pie Town homesteads
succeed. Yet, New Deal agricultural policy was designed to pro-
mote technical efficiency and progress, not preserve the local communities and family traditions of rural America. The FSA's man-
date was to assist the poorest farmers; and some of its programs,
like grants and loans to small farmers, were designed to ease their
suffering, but the FSA's underlying belief was that these small farmers were eventually going to move to the cities. Rather than exam-
ine the cause of the Caudills' deprivation and suffering by examin-
ing the government programs that displaced tenant farmers or wondering whether homesteading on the wind-swept and arid Continental Divide of New Mexico was a practical solution to those who
were poor and homeless, Lee's Pie Town photographs make the
Caudills' poverty attractive. They intimate that Doris and Faro's
struggles were the result of a Job-like misfortune rather than consequences of political and economic decisions mandated by a changing economy and government programs.

When I ask Jean Lee how she feels about the photographs these
many years later, she hesitates for a moment and then looks me in
the eye as she says:

We knew these people probably couldn't make it. That land
shouldn't ever have been stirred with a stick. There was no good
topsoil, none at all.

Actually, we really shouldn't ever have taken a photograph in
Pie Town. They give a false impression. It was such a desperate
period, but this was no answer. It was interesting, the way they
were living in dugouts with no electricity, no telephones or running

water. It appealed to people elsewhere in the country. It was a nostalgia thing even then. It appealed to everybody, to Stryker, to the magazines.

How does Doris feel about Lee's portrayal of her family's time in Divide? I ask her whether Lee's photographs show the life she remembers. At first she says they do, but the next moment she begins to qualify her answer. She remembers so many more events and people than he photographed. What about the time May Potter ran off with Dudd Hart in the middle of the night, and May's father heard her leave and ran after the couple in the snow to tell them he felt fine about them getting married? What about the pie suppers just before Christmas? She also says that Lee's photographs show amenities that were signs of a financial stability that her family did not achieve. She looks at a photograph of Mrs. Hutton with a homemade washing machine and tells me that they did not have such conveniences out where they lived. The Huttons were latecomers who had enough money to buy a proved-up homestead and came with comfortable furniture. They lived north of Pie Town and were not true hard-core homesteaders like those who lived in the far harsher reality of Divide. "All that was like a different world from us."

Doris lived the reality that Lee photographed, however, and she for the most part believes the myth. Despite the deprivation, her homesteading years are a luminous memory for her.

I just want to help you all I can. It's not that important to us because we're through with it, but somewhere down the line are other generations, who are going to wonder about these things. Just like us enjoying books about when the pilgrims came over and set up the thirteen original colonies. Names aren't that important, except that to someone they will be their grandparents. It won't be in my lifetime or yours but on down the line. That's important. It's part of our heritage.

The wrench of leaving "made Faro a little crazy." For Doris, pulling up stakes after ten years tore out a piece of her heart. It made her nostalgic. It made her, albeit some years later, determined to tell her story.

Today, Catron County has fallen on hard times. Only seventy post-office boxes serve the entire Pie Town region. For serious shopping or to go to a movie, one must drive sixty-five miles north on dirt roads to Grants, eighty-five miles east to Socorro or seventy-five miles west to Springerville, Arizona. There is still no doctor in Pie Town. Farming has become increasingly difficult with the decrease in average yearly rainfall. Roy McKee, one of the few who stuck it out, harvested his last bean crop in 1956, and then took up well drilling to survive. Gradually, a few individuals and large corporations bought up the small ranches. Many ranchers took to raising stock, but today the price of beef is low, and the costs of raising cattle have risen steadily. Today, most owners do not live in the area, and with the economics of the large ranches and modern equipment, few hired hands are needed. Little work can be found in the entire county.

Although new residents have moved in during the last few years, they are of a different time and ethos than Doris, Faro, and their generation, and they live in far different economic circumstances. Even if they have moved to Pie Town with a naïve optimism that disregards the harsh climate, scarcity of water, and lack of community services, it is unlikely that they will find the romance that Lee photographed and Doris keeps alive in her memories and her stories. The frontier Pie Town has vanished, and only the traces left by a few written recollections, a few snapshots, and the wonderful mythic story told by Russell Lee's photographs remain in testimony to those brief moments and the resolute homesteaders who made them.

AFTERWORD

Photographs tell very short stories, a moment's worth. My full-face portrait of Doris Caudill, homesteader, taken at one two-hundred-and-fiftieth of a second, does not show a girl of fifteen wearing stylish lounging pajamas and laughing in front of the Pie Town, New Mexico, Hotel in 1929. But that was Doris once, in another moment. She has a family snapshot to prove it. She has also kept a tattered copy of *U.S. Camera* from 1941 that shows her as government photographer Russell Lee pictured her in 1940, a wife and mother living with a group of other hardy souls in a small New Mexico homesteading community.

These three sorts of photographic images coexist: Lee's professional images of Doris on her homestead, Doris's family snapshots from the same period, and my photographs of Doris and the homesteading area fifty years later. No single image tells a complete story. Even as a group, they cannot capture all of it. Each picture of Doris captures a split second in her life. What happened before or after the shutter was tripped cannot be glimpsed. What took place outside the camera viewfinder left no trace on film.

For those who appear in the photographs, the memories of moments photographed do not always match the images. Their memories are more expansive than photographs, and they remember events differently. Their history is a rich tapestry of interrelated feelings, sensory input, and events woven through time. In addition, those who appear look back at photographs taken decades before with eyes accustomed to more recent conventions of photographic representation. Doris's daughter Josie hates the photos that Russell Lee made of her and her mother and friends. They all look solemn, she says. "I never did feel like that. Mother, you never looked like that, either. That's horrible! To think that people would actually print something like that!"

Russell Lee's work, even though he used handheld cameras and the newfangled flashbulbs, came from a nineteenth-century tradition, where the portrait was a special occasion and solemnity seemed appropriate. One's soul was not to be treated with levity, and smiling portraits were reserved for the insane and the dissolute. Although Lee's images depict informal situations, they were carefully planned and frequently posed. He used images of daily life to reflect larger cultural issues and he preferred that his subjects not smile when he photographed them. As a result, his images may long outlive their subjects but were not always appreciated by them.

Doris's snapshots are full of smiling friends and relatives. With the advent of snapshot cameras and faster film, people could, for the first time in history, make their own family pictures. They could represent themselves. Gradually the smile became more common. Doris's snapshots are mostly out of focus and loosely framed, with a tree protruding from Aunt Julia's head or a dog half out of the picture. However, what they lack in elegance they more than make up for in intimacy. Josie handles them with respect and affection. They record happy moments: the day a family member visited or a new calf was born.

When I photograph Doris on our first meeting at Cascade Locks, I, like Lee, ask her not to smile. I want her simply to relax and look into the lens. But she is conscious that Lee photographed her that way more than half a century ago. She worries that I will photograph her looking grim and out of character. What will Josie think when she sees a mother who looks like she has lost her last friend?

"I don't want to look sad, " Doris says. "I've always been full of the devil."

The experience of photographing Doris and her Pie Town homestead, which I had seen in Lee's photos and Doris's snapshots, led me to consider the choices that photographers make when they "take a picture." That eye-blink click of the shutter is an act of intention. Each of us has an agenda, however conscious, when we depress the camera shutter. Lee was salaried to produce images for a government agency. Doris's family wanted to make keepsakes for a family album. I took pictures to document the vestiges of a story that happened long ago. The scene is recorded but the agenda of the photographer is not.

Though the camera clicks in fractions of a second (an apt recording instrument for a country like ours that has existed in a perpetual present tense), the framed moment it captures lasts forever. Both Lee's and Doris's photographs have survived more than half a century, and the moments they record have become timeless. Gradually, both the intentions of the photographer and the environment around the frame have been forgotten. Russell Lee died in 1987, and the government agency he worked for is no longer in operation. Few of his subjects are alive to contradict his presentation of them or to tell their own stories. Lee's photographs, despite his wife Jean's detailed captions, have lost much of their documentary context and become valued as art objects.

Lee's images, along with others by photographers such as Dorothea Lange, Marion Post Wolcott, and Arthur Rubenstein have become hallmark images for how we think of rural America during the Depression. How accurate was Lee's depiction of Pie Town? What elements of homesteading life did he leave out? What about Doris's snapshots? Does their spontaneity contribute an immediacy that Lee's images do not? How do snapshots and more polished professional images work together to provide a rich trove of information about a particular time, place, and culture?

With Doris as storyteller and guide, I have had a rare opportunity to explore these questions. When I photographed, I used my camera like an archaeologist slowly digging a site, photographing the few scraps of rusty metal and cracked wood that are all that remain from the life Doris once led in arid Pie Town. In the text, I juxtaposed history, photographs, and recollections, as well as describing Doris as she is today. In the process of telling her story, I found I had an agenda of my own: to tell her story, a woman's story, without the usual romance that Hollywood and the Western novel have led us to attach to homesteading in the American West.

Not only did I photograph Doris's homestead, I also walked the fields where she pulled rabbitbrush and weeded bean rows. I nibbled lamb's quarter and sheep sorrel. I squatted down and drew in the same dirt that her daughter Josie kneaded and formed into mud pies fifty-five years earlier. My photographs, I found, were far less interesting or informational than the experiences I had while visiting her and her homestead. My adventures, though less demanding and exciting than her own, did provide a tactile means of measuring Lee's photos and Doris's snapshots against a reality of my own experience.

Photography is like personal reminiscence in that it can be evocative and vividly detailed. It can provide valuable historical information unavailable from any other source. Indeed, photography *is* history in visual form. However, like storytelling, photography is so highly selective in its presentation of history that its truths always necessitate questioning. In today's era of digital imaging with our ability to invisibly alter an image, we are learning to be more suspicious of what we see in the media, but we need to reexamine historical images as well. Photography with its appearance of verisimilitude can lie more convincingly than any other medium. History, as Jean Cocteau once noted, has always been a mixture of reality and fantasy, where "the unreality of the fable becomes the truth."

NOTES

Notes on Sources

Numerous articles and books have helped me understand the homesteading era in New Mexico, and Pie Town in particular. Chief among them were Donald Worster's *Dust Bowl: The Southern Plains in the 1930s* (New York: Oxford University Press, 1979); Jerry L. William's *New Mexico in Maps*. 2nd ed. (Albuquerque: University of New Mexico Press, 1986); Agnes Morley Cleaveland's *No Life for a Lady* (Lincoln: University of Nebraska Press, 1977); Paul Bonnifield's *The Dust Bowl: Men, Dirt and Depression* (Albuquerque: University of New Mexico Press, 1979); *New Mexicans in Cameo and Camera: New Deal Documentation of Twentieth-Century Lives*, Marta Weigle, ed. (Albuquerque: University of New Mexico Press, 1985); *The Lore of New Mexico* (Albuquerque: University of New Mexico Press, 1988) by Marta Weigle and Peter White; and *The New Deal: The State and Local Levels*, 2 vols., John Braeman, Robert H. Bremner, and David Brody, eds. (Columbus: Ohio State University Press, 1975). Helpful for understanding the role of women in the homesteading era were Marta Weigle: *Essays on Rural Women* (Albuquerque: University of New Mexico Press, 1991), and her upublished manuscript "Homesteading on the Zuni Plateau" (1979).

For Pie Town, Kathryn McKee Roberts's *From the Top of the Mountain: Pie Town, New Mexico, and Neighbors!* (Albuquerque: Roger Coffin, 1990) was invaluable. Also important were the following articles: Toby Smith, "Pie Town: A Trip Back," *Impact Magazine, Albuquerque Journal*, 18 January 1983; Larry Meyer's "Pie Town: Last Homesteading Community," *Inn America*, reprinted from *American Heritage* 31 (February/March 1980): 74–81; "Return to Pie Town," *Albuquerque Tribune*, 22 August 1996 with photos by KayLynn Deveney and story by Ollie Reed Jr.; and the exhibition catalogue *Retracing Russell Lee's Steps: A New Documentary* (Southwest Texas State University, 1991).

Many fine books have been written on the FSA and the photographers of the New Deal era. Most valuable to me were F. Jack Hurley's *A Portrait of a Decade: Roy Stryker and the Development of Documentary Photography in the Thirties* (Baton Rouge: Louisiana State University Press, 1972); Hank O'Neal's *A Vision Shared: A Classic Portrait of America and Its People, 1935–1943* (New York: St. Martin's Press, 1976); *Documenting America, 1935–1943*, Carl Fleischhauer and Beverly W. Brannan, eds. (Berkeley: University of California Press, 1988); Arthur Rothstein's *Documentary Photography* (Stoneham, Mass.: Focal Press, 1986); Maren Stange's *Symbols of Ideal Life: Social Documentary Photography in America, 1890–1950* (Cambridge: University of Cambridge Press, 1992); *Official Images: New Deal Photography*, Pete Daniel, Merry A. Foresta, Maren Stange, and Sally Stein, eds. (Washington, D.C.: Smithsonian Institution Press, 1987); Bill Ganzel's *Dust Bowl Descent* (Lincoln: University of Nebraska Press, 1984); and Nancy Wood's *Heartland New Mexico: Photographs from the Farm Security Administration, 1935–1943* (Albuquerque: University of New Mexico Press, 1989). Important articles included "Not Intended for Framing: The FSA Archive," by Edwin Rosskam in *Afterimage* (March 1981): 9–11. I also used and have quoted from Roy Stryker's correspondence with Russell Lee found in *The Roy Stryker Papers* from the University of Louisville Archives and Record Center.

Frank Hurley's *Russell Lee, Photographer* (Dobbs Ferry, N.Y.: Morgan & Morgan, 1978) is the most complete biography of Russell Lee. Lee's photographs of Pie Town with uncredited captions and text by Jean Lee appeared in "Life on the American Frontier—1941 Version," *U.S. Camera* (October 1941). I obtained additional information from *Russell Lee's FSA Photographs of Chamisal and Peñasco, New Mexico*, William Wroth, ed. (Santa Fe: Ancient City Press, 1985); the Russell Lee Collection, 1903–1986, from the Southwestern Writers Collection, Southwest Texas State University, San Marcos, Texas; and from Ann Mundy's fine documentary *Photographer: Russell Lee* (Austin: Ann Mundy & Associates, Film & Video Productions, 1987).

My interviews with Doris Jackson (formerly Doris Caudill), 1995–98, and her handwritten memoir "Pie Town, New Mexico" are the basis for the numerous quotations and references in my text. Other information came from interviews with Roy McKee, 1995–98, Sam McKee, 1995, Geneva McKee Younger, 1995, Jackie Barrington, 1995, Colita Schalbar and Loraine Burns, 1996, Kathryn McKee Roberts, 1996–98, and current residents of Pie Town, 1995–97. Although I had the pleasure of meeting Russell Lee briefly, he died before I began this project. My interview with Jean Lee took place in May 1996, a few months before she died.

Chapter Notes

1. Mary Powell of Ancient City Press shared this correspondence with me with the permission of Marta Weigle, the editor of *Women of New Mexico: Depression Era Images* (Santa Fe: Ancient City Press, 1993). Marta wrote a short account of Doris's life, entitled "Pie Town: A slice of homestead life," for *New Mexico Magazine* (November 1996). Because of my interest in Pie Town, I agreed to photograph Doris for the article. After meeting her in June 1995, I spoke with Marta and she agreed that I might do a book-length treatment of Doris's life in Pie Town. Doris was most enthusiastic about both projects.

2. Alegra Mountain is the local term for

the mountain and has been used throughout this text. The current accepted name is Alegres Mountain, set by the United States Board on Geographic Names.

3. All quotations from Doris Caudill (now Doris Jackson) have been taken from her forty-six page, hand-written memoir given to the author at the June 1995 meeting and from telephone and personal interviews from June 1995 to January 2000.

4. John Steinbeck, *Grapes of Wrath* (New York: Penguin Books, 1967), 541–42.

5. Agnes Morley Cleaveland, *No Life for a Lady* (Lincoln: University of Nebraska Press, 1977), 332–33.

6. Larry Meyer, "Pie Town," *Inn America*, reprinted from *American Heritage* 31 (February/March 1980): 81–82.

7. Meyer, "Pie Town," 82.

8. Author's interviews with Roy McKee in June and August 1995. Roy died 9 May 2000.

9. Meyer, "Pie Town," 82.

10. Sally Stein, "FSA Color: The Forgotten Document," *Modern Photography* (January 1979): 93.

11. Nancy Wood, *Heartland New Mexico: Photographs from the Farm Security Administration, 1935–1943* (Albuquerque: University of New Mexico Press, 1989), 24.

12. Author's interview with Loraine Burns and Colita Schalbar, 17 June 1996.

13. Branch water is how they referred to the minimal amount of water available to them. It refers metaphorically to the water from tiny streams feeding a larger river.

14. All of the Stryker-Lee correspondence quoted comes from *The Roy Stryker Papers: Series I—Correspondence,* from the University of Louisville Archives and Record Center. The date of the letter accompanies each quotation.

15. Frank Hurley, *Russell Lee: Photographer* (Dobbs Ferry, New York: Morgan & Morgan, 1979), 15.

16. Edwin Rosskam, "Not Intended for Framing: The FSA Archive," *Afterimage* (March 1981): 9.

17. Russell Lee, interview with Richard K. Doud for the Archives of American Art, 2 June 1964, quoted in *Russell Lee's FSA Photographs of Chamisal and Penasco, New Mexico*, William Wroth, ed. (Santa Fe: Ancient City Press, 1985), 125–26.

18. Author's interview with Jean Lee, 16 May 1996.

19. Russell Lee, "Life on the American Frontier—1941 Version," *U.S. Camera* (October 1941): 89.

20. "Russell Lee's works donated to UT center," *American Statesman*, 29 August 1986.

21. Obituary, privately printed, for Jean Lee, 22 October 1996.

22. James Curtis, *Mind's Eye, Mind's Truth: FSA Photography Reconsidered* (Philadelphia: Temple University Press, 1989), 110.

23. Author's interview with Jean Lee, May 1996. Jean Lee passed away 19 October 1996.

24. Wood, *Heartland New Mexico*, 10.

25. *Roy Stryker Papers,* Stryker to Lee, 19 September 1940.

26. Lee, "Life on the American Frontier," 107.

27. Interview with Colita Schalbar, 17 June 1996.

28. Lee, "Life on the American Frontier," 88.

29. Author's letter from Josie Caudill Endsley, October 1995.

30. Lee, "Life on the American Frontier," 88.

31. Lee, "Life on the American Frontier," 107.

PHOTOGRAPHS BY JOAN MYERS

Pie Town today

Pie Town Hotel, where Russell and Jean Lee stayed

Very Large Array on the plains of St. Augustine

Car near Divide school building

Divide school teacherage

Divide cemetery

Road adjoining the Caudill homestead

Site where Doris and Faro lived when they were first married

Fred ("Pop") Caudill's dugout

Site of final Caudill dugout where water was found